RIT - WALLACE LIBRARY
CIRCULATING LIBRARY BOOKS

OVERDUE FINES AND FEES FOR <u>ALL</u> BORROWERS

- Recalled = $1/ day overdue (no grace period)
- Billed = $10.00/ item when returned 4 or more weeks overdue
- Lost Items = replacement cost+$10 fee
- All materials must be returned or renewed by the duedate.

THOROGOOD
PROFESSIONAL
INSIGHTS

A SPECIALLY COMMISSIONED REPORT

SURVIVING A CORPORATE CRISIS

100 THINGS YOU NEED TO KNOW

Paul Batchelor

THOROGOOD

THOROGOOD
PROFESSIONAL
INSIGHTS

A SPECIALLY COMMISSIONED REPORT

SURVIVING A CORPORATE CRISIS

100 THINGS YOU NEED TO KNOW

Paul Batchelor

THOROGOOD

Other Thorogood Professional Insights

Successfully Defending Employment Tribunal Cases

Dennis Hunt

Managing Corporate Reputation

Susan Croft and John Dalton

Successful Competitive Tendering

Jeff Woodhams

The Legal Protection of Databases

Simon Chalton

The Internet and E-Commerce

Peter Carey

Technical Aspects of Business Leases

Malcolm Dowden

The Commercial Exploitation of Intellectual Property Rights by Licensing

Charles D. DesForges

The Competition Act – Practical Advice and Guidance

Susan Singleton

Special discounts for bulk quantities of Thorogood books are available to corporations, institutions, associations and other organisations. For more information contact Thorogood by telephone on 020 7749 4748, by fax on 020 7729 6110, or e-mail us: info@thorogood.ws

Published by Thorogood
10-12 Rivington Street
London EC2A 3DU.

t: 020 7749 4748

f: 020 7729 6110

e: info@thorogood.ws

w: www.thorogood.ws

A CIP catalogue record for this Report is available from the British Library.

ISBN 1 85418 208 0

Printed in Great Britain by printflow.com

About the Author

Paul Batchelor is a Fellow of the Association of Chartered Certified Accountants and a Freeman of the City of London. Currently a Director of Professional Interim Management Services Limited, he has almost twenty years experience in senior roles in the U.K. retail financial services sector, recently specialising in internal audit, compliance, special investigations and risk management. He also has substantial experience in management accounting, treasury and strategic planning.

Over a five-year period, Paul was responsible for creating, maintaining and testing the business resumption planning capabilities of a leading U.K. financial services group.

At a time when the threat to business stability has never been greater, he has drawn on this experience to produce a Report that sets out the basic principles of crisis management for all businesses. The report is aimed at senior management. It guides the reader through the various stages of setting up a viable corporate crisis response capability and provides a series of 'key questions' that every Chief Executive Officer or Managing Director should want to ask – and that every Corporate Crisis Manager should be able to answer.

Paul was a member of the U.K. financial services society committee of a major international accounting body for ten years, serving as Vice-Chairman and Deputy Chairman over a four-year period and Chairman for three years.

Contents

APPENDICES   91

Introduction
– The purpose of this Report

This report is designed primarily for those directors and senior managers who are concerned that their organisations may not be adequately prepared to deal effectively with the unthinkable – a corporate crisis that threatens the very existence of their business. It will also be of use to officers who are charged personally with maintaining crisis management systems, if only to prepare them for the questions that they will be asked once their seniors have read the report.

> *Seven out of ten organisations that experience a corporate crisis go out of business within 18 months.*

Whilst this is a sobering statistic, I am sure that your interest will be focused entirely on the fact that you would expect to be amongst the three survivors. After all, failure is the sort of thing that happens to other people, isn't it?

Well, actually, no it isn't. Failure happens to businesses that are not prepared; businesses that have not subjected themselves to the disciplines of planning, training, controlling and exercising those routines that could spell the difference between corporate life and death in a crisis situation.

But it isn't just about life and death, it's about damage limitation, minimising impact and restoring the status quo with as little delay as possible. To use modern corporate governance speak, it's about safeguarding the organisation's assets and protecting its shareholders. Ultimately, though, it's about keeping your job.

Let's take a step back, for a moment, and consider the following questions:

A major crisis has affected your organisation:

- How would you find out about it?
- What do you do?
- Where do you go?
- Who do you talk to?
- Who do you listen to?
- Who would be in charge?

Before you answer the above questions, think about the state of mind you and your colleagues would be in, should the worst happen. You may well concede that this would not actually be the best time to draw up plans to deal with the crisis. Likewise, it would be little better to have to take a dust-covered Business Resumption Plan from the shelf and read it for the first time.

Think of how many things you do automatically when driving your car – things that you are so experienced in doing that they can be consigned to the back of your mind, leaving you to concentrate fully on the unexpected hazards that form part of every journey.

How many times have you got out of your car at the end of a familiar journey and thought to yourself 'I don't remember coming along that stretch of road', or, 'I don't recall such-and-such a junction'? When, in fact, you know you **did** negotiate those obstacles as part of the journey. It means you were driving 'on autopilot'; thinking about something else. Why? Because, you were so familiar with the exercise that you demoted it from the front-line of your consciousness – the training had 'kicked in'.

I'm not suggesting that you should be able to handle a corporate crisis while concentrating on something else. Rather, I am making the point that when you are handling something as complex as driving a car, or managing a corporate crisis, you are more likely to be successful if you've done it before, know what to expect and don't have to worry about where everything is.

> *When it comes down to handling a corporate crisis, you are only likely to have one shot at it in your career – and that's if you are unlucky. You would have to be very, very unlucky to experience more than one major workplace crisis. So, how can you know what to expect?*

You can call it training, drilling, exercising or, simply, being prepared; but that's what you need – regular exposure to the problems. It's inconvenient and it takes valuable time, but it has to be done, otherwise, some jaywalker is going to walk right in front of your corporate crisis routine when you're not looking and bring the whole business to a violent standstill.

Now, back to those questions. If you can answer all of them without hesitation, and are confident that all of the key people in your organisation could do likewise, then you may not need this Report. Pass it on to a colleague (if you are not **totally** confident), or a competitor (if you are feeling charitable).

On the other hand, if you hesitated or couldn't answer one or more of the questions, or felt that your colleagues might have displayed uncertainty if faced with the same questions, then this Report may be of some help to you and them.

The Report is not a checklist for dealing with a crisis, although it may well help you build such a list. It is a common-sense, jargon-free journey through the building blocks that need to be assembled to enable you to sleep nights, safe in the knowledge that you have done everything possible to ensure that your business would not only survive a crisis, but would recover as quickly as possible with the minimum loss of value and public relations backlash.

Use this Report as a reference point. Each chapter concludes with a list of 'Key Questions' that the senior executive can use either to impress his subordinates, by demonstrating his grasp of crisis management, or, more importantly, as a means of cutting through the detail to gain (and give) assurance that all is well. Should you have misgivings when faced with the answers, use the Key Questions to instruct your internal review team to look into the subject.

The Report itself will help you make sense of the answers you **do** receive **and** give you the confidence to direct changes where necessary. Here are a few to get you going:

Things you need to know...

KEY QUESTIONS

1 Could the business be vulnerable to an unexpected event, whether natural or man-made?

2 Would the sudden loss of staff/management resources cause disruption to the business?

3 Would the business suffer greatly as a result of prolonged and unexpected denial of access to its main premises?

4 Would general IT failure cause major problems to the business?

5 Is there a Corporate Crisis Management Plan to deal with the above eventualities?

6 Who is responsible for the Plan?

7 What is your role in the Plan?

8 Is the plan ever tested?

THOROGOOD
PROFESSIONAL
INSIGHTS

Chapter 1

Starting at the beginning – crisis avoidance

Chapter 1

Starting at the beginning
– crisis avoidance

The first rule of crisis management has got to be 'crisis avoidance'.

We are all familiar with the expression 'attack is the best form of defence'. We can use internal controls to attack many of the causes of possible crises and rewrite that expression to read: **'(crisis) avoidance is the best form of (crisis) management'**.

Internal controls

There is no point in pretending that it is possible to take steps to avoid every eventuality – we have all learned that is not the case – sometimes from bitter experience. What we do know, however, is that there is no need to 'leave the stable door open'. Risk management and internal control systems can go a long way towards preventing problems which could escalate into crises and we need to ensure that the appropriate controls are in place and effective.

Board responsibilities

It is the Board's responsibility to identify, assess and understand the risks faced by the business, and to ensure that internal control systems are in place, effective and adequate to deal with them. Many of the risks that might lead to corporate crises ought to be identified during the Board's strategic planning deliberations – although, of course, this does not include freak accidents. Natural disasters could fall into either camp, dependent upon whether they can be reasonably foreseen. In risk terms, it depends upon their level of probability or likelihood.

As an example, an organisation whose factory is situated on a flood plain should have identified the risk of flooding as a threat in its SWOT analysis (Strengths, Weaknesses, Opportunities, Threats), which should form part of the strategic planning process. This being the case, we would expect the internal control system to include documented contingency plans for dealing with a flood. We might

also expect controls ensuring the maintenance of flood prevention and detection systems, although our ability to prevent natural disasters is limited and any preventive controls might be focused on limiting the damage caused by flooding, rather than preventing the flood itself.

Internal and external risks

Whilst there are exceptions, it would seem that the majority of 'killer risks' would be externally generated, so, from the 'crisis avoidance' perspective, it makes sense to differentiate between internally and externally generated risks. In the case of the former, whilst there may be a significant number of them, internal controls should be robust enough to **prevent** a high proportion of the events that **could** lead to a crisis, and **detect** most of the remainder, so that **limitation** action can be taken before these events get out-of-hand. In the case of externally generated risks, fewer but more deadly, prevention may take a back seat to detection, although, in many cases, it might be too late to be helpful (Figure 1).

The domino effect

Whilst it is true that internally generated risks are likely to be manageable and, for the most part, fairly minor, we must not forget the 'domino effect' that can turn a minor event into a major corporate crisis, if mis-handled.

I suppose Barings is the ultimate example of such a situation. Although it could be argued that this was, in fact, an example of a rare 'blockbuster' internal event in an industry where such major risks are possible, there can be no doubt that it was the crystallisation of external risk that finally closed the bank down.

Nearer to home, I give a fictitious example of a savings bank employee who steals from customers' accounts. When one of the misappropriations comes to light, it is inevitably reported in the media. The worst-case scenario is that it is badly reported and mis-handled by bank management to such an extent that savers lose confidence in the bank and close their accounts in droves. This process reveals a few more cases of missing funds and the bank has difficulty satisfying the huge volume of demand for cash, as customers rush to get their life-savings out of (what they perceive to be) an unsafe environment. This is reported in the media and the exodus gathers momentum. If confidence cannot be restored, it is likely that the bank's share price will fall dramatically and it will have to be rescued, or taken over.

This, then, is an example of a fairly minor internally generated event getting out-of-hand and leading to a major corporate crisis.

The moral is clear: **Maintain your internal control systems to prevent and detect events that might otherwise become uncontrollable**.

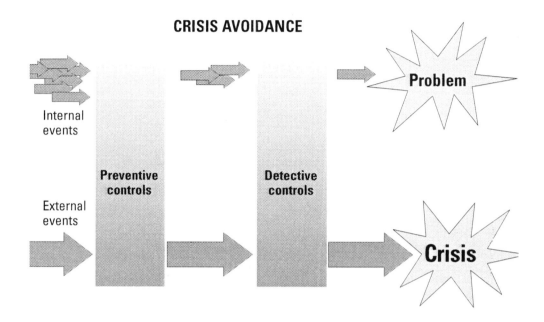

Figure 1: *Internal Events are easier to avoid than External Events*

When avoidance is not an option

If you were to put a group of people in a room and ask them to come up with a scheme that would eliminate the risk of a jumbo-jet accidentally falling out of the sky onto their headquarters building, you would probably find that most of the schemes offered would expose the headquarters building to risks far greater than those which you were seeking to avoid. All would probably have an adverse effect on the conduct of business.

Examples might include the following:

- **Encase the building in a shell of sufficiently thick reinforced concrete** (the Bunker approach).

- **Build an underwater headquarters** (the Relocation approach).

- **Ban all flights** (the Luddite approach).

- **Set up the headquarters on a space station above the flying altitude of jumbo-jets** (the Final Frontier approach).

The objective of the above is not to inject levity into an otherwise stressful subject, but to open the debate on likelihood and the cost/benefit implications of risk control. Quite simply, you cannot, in commercial terms, totally eliminate the risk referred to above. You might advise against relocating to a building that is situated on the approach path of an airport, but that is as far as you would go.

This is the case with many externally generated risks – particularly those with such a low likelihood.

Contingency plans

One of the early lessons in the study of operational risk management is that low likelihood/high impact risks require contingency plans. Such plans represent the bedrock of effective crisis management.

Likelihood is a strange concept. When looked at in relation to the probability that a jumbo-jet might fall on your headquarters building (and leaving aside deliberate acts of terrorism), whilst you might concede that it is possible, you have to conclude that the risk is negligible. In other words, the likelihood is very, very, very low and you don't need a specific contingency plan. On the other hand, if your factory is built on a flood plain, what is the likelihood of you suffering a flood? Past records may indicate that floods might be expected once every ten years and the local authority may have recently improved its flood defences, thus making a catastrophe less probable. Does this make the probability as low as the jumbo-jet falling out of the sky? The answer, of course, is 'no'. Whilst the likelihood of a flood may be low, it remains exponentially higher than a jumbo-jet accident – the business needs a contingency plan to cover this specific risk.

Accident, crime, politics, terrorism, insurrection, hostilities and natural disasters.

These are the risks that are most likely to lead to major corporate crises. Whilst many of them will be externally generated, we must ensure that the limited controls available to us to prevent or detect their crystallisation are in place and effective.

Changing risks

In the latter part of the 20th century, businesses focused on specific types of crisis:

Denial of premises or denial of computer services

There was then an emphasis on terrorist activity, which has, if anything, grown as we have moved into the 21st century. Concerns that had been largely limited to localised areas like the U.K., where IRA operations in the larger cities had brought chaos to business communities, were now worldwide issues following dreadful attacks in the United States and Bali.

Hostage situations were also seen as possibilities, although these required a different approach to those crises that actually interrupted business.

There was always the fear that hackers might infiltrate computer systems, denying service and therefore affecting the organisation's day-to-day business. This fear has now been augmented by the widespread use of web-based technology and the demonstrable ease with which control systems can be by-passed, to the detriment of both the business and its customers.

Basic controls

In spite of all this, there are still a number of common sense measures that organisations should consider putting in place to either prevent problems or mitigate their effects:

- **Clear desk policy** – don't leave papers around to be stolen/photocopied by criminals or destroyed in a fire or blast.

- **Confidential waste policy** – shred papers that could be used to damage your business if they get into the wrong hands.

- **Secure buildings policy** – controlled access to and egress from buildings for staff and visitors; CCTV on doors and boundaries; tighter security for sensitive areas such as computer rooms; blast protection on windows.

- **Computer security policy** – up to date anti-virus software; screened Internet access; restrictions on computer access and data transfer by employees.

- **Disaster standby facilities** – backup computer systems; standby production and clerical resources; available finances.

- **Staff controls** – know where absent key staff members are at any given time; restrictions on key staff members travelling together on business.

The above are just a few examples of the sort of measures that should be part and parcel of an effective internal control system. When viewed in isolation, their importance is obvious.

Remember:

- Prevention is better than cure.
- Avoiding your crisis is better than managing it.

Things you need to know...

**CRISIS AVOIDANCE
KEY QUESTIONS**

9   Does the organisation comply with regulatory requirements on internal control?

10   Who reports to the Board on internal control compliance?

11   Is the internal control system fully in place?

12   How is the internal control system monitored/tested?

13   Is there a clear desk policy?

14   Is there a confidential waste policy?

15   Is there a secure buildings policy?

16   Is there a computer security policy?

17   Are there disaster standby facilities?

18   Is there a key staff location system?

19   Are there any specific contingency plans?

20   Has the possible effect of terrorist attack been taken seriously in considering the above points?

THOROGOOD

PROFESSIONAL

INSIGHTS

Chapter 2

Defining crisis management strategy

Defining crisis management strategy

You must have a Board-approved crisis management strategy.

Support from the very top of the organisation is essential if the crisis administrators are to be effective in changing the culture of the management team and obtaining the necessary budget approvals to build the infrastructure that will be so important in the event of a major problem.

What is a crisis?

The strategy should define the word **crisis**, in corporate terms. In other words, the Board should start by setting out its stall as to what types of event, and extents of disruption/damage are covered by the strategy.

This section might start with a general definition, such as: '**Any event that threatens the continuation of the organisation or its ability to attain its corporate objectives.**' This, however, requires more detail, which might take the form of statements of guidance that show that the Board understands the risks faced by the business. The Board will need to have clear ideas on what would turn a localised problem into a crisis. What are the trigger points?

- Cost?
- Duration?
- Extent?
- Reputational impact?

Cost

Looking at 'cost', a bank Board might take the view that a sudden diminution in its asset value, or a sudden increase in its liabilities, above a certain level, should be regarded as a corporate crisis. The Barings debacle makes this point particularly well:

A bank trader, operating overseas in the derivatives markets, committed the bank to liabilities above and beyond his mandates – more importantly, market movements (the externally generated killer risk, in this scenario) took the commitments above and beyond the bank's ability to honour them. That this was a crisis is self-evident – the bank failed as a result – but was the possibility of such a crisis recognised in advance and planned for? The questions surrounding preventive and detective controls, coupled with the availability and use of relevant and timely management information in this case have filled many pages, but for our purpose it exemplifies the crisis potential of sudden, unexpected, major costs.

Duration

'Duration' is another important element of the equation. It might be argued that if Barings could have quietly worked through its liabilities over, say, a five-year period, and without public scrutiny, it could have survived. Sadly, that was not an option – the markets required immediate settlement, or the confidence that this was possible.

Taking another example, a Board might look at IT service provision and take the view that, if the organisation's computer systems go down during business hours, there should be (say) a three hour period before a corporate crisis is declared. Obviously, such considerations would depend upon the extent to which the conduct of business is reliant upon the computer and the availability of standby systems. Similar considerations apply to denial of access to premises. A three-hour denial caused by a bomb hoax or a fire alarm, might be something that the organisation would take in its stride and deal with as an operational inconvenience. On the other hand, the possibility of denial for 24 hours with no certainty of a return to normality would be categorised as a corporate crisis by most Boards.

Extent

This is fairly straightforward. If an organisation that has over 100 retail outlets loses one of them, it might take the view that there is a perfectly viable contingency plan for such an event and there is no need to call a corporate crisis. The contingency plan might involve the Services and Operations Departments working together to relocate the business of that particular outlet and keep its customers informed. In fact, such an episode might be 'spun' to demonstrate the organisation's resilience – as long as it all went smoothly. The situation would, of course, be more serious if (say) a cluster of five outlets were lost simultaneously.

Reputational impact

This can be the most damaging element. Otherwise insignificant events can be magnified out of all proportion once reputation is questioned. A Board will be aware that reputational impact can accrue from many situations and it is important that a management team recognises the danger signs early enough to take whatever countermeasures are available. When defining its position on reputational impact, a Board would do well to acknowledge the seriousness of this element and leave its management team to declare a crisis at the earliest possible point in time.

Crisis trigger points

Whatever measures the Board uses to indicate the trigger points at which corporate crisis mechanisms should be invoked, it must acknowledge the right of management to declare a crisis in advance of those points being reached. The thresholds stated in the strategy document should, therefore, be the points at which crisis mechanisms **must** be invoked – earlier invocation is management's only option – exceeding the trigger points is likely to be considered dereliction of duty and the strategy document should make this clear.

Infrastructure

Board strategy should specify the crisis management infrastructure, that is to say the mechanisms with which a crisis will be handled – the framework that will be employed. This will include the teams that will be called upon, their authority and responsibilities, and the reporting mechanisms that will apply.

Mission

In view of the fact that crisis mechanisms will take precedence over normal line relationships, the strategy needs to delimit the duration of their existence, so as to make it clear when those normal relationships will be resumed. To this end, the crisis management mission should be clearly defined. It might include the following words:

- Work (with the authorities) to neutralise the crisis event and limit escalation.

- Protect the organisation's assets and staff.

- Safeguard the organisation's reputation.

- Authorise remedial works/temporary solutions.

- Oversee the resumption of normal business activities.

- Hand overall control back to line management on completion of the above.

The above are self-explanatory, but the first bullet point acknowledges that, in many situations, the crisis management team will have to work with (and, in some cases, under the direction of) the emergency services. This will inevitably mean that there will be times when public safety will take precedence over the corporate crisis mission statement. This is unavoidable and it is therefore essential that crisis leaders do everything possible to forge close relationships with those in charge of the emergency services on site, in the hope that some consideration will be given to the plight of the business when borderline decisions need to be made.

Of course, you might just get lucky, as was the case with a large U.K. insurance company that was denied access to its offices following a terrorist-bombing incident. The offices had been very badly damaged and the police had thrown an exclusion cordon all around the site – nobody was allowed in, apart from the authorities. This situation was causing the insurance company some distress, as

can be imagined. They had no idea how long the denial of access would continue and there were a number of important documents within the premises, which required urgent action. As a last resort, somebody (let's call him the insurance company's crisis administrator) produced to the police an extract from the Business Resumption Manual, which stated that **'in the event of a crisis, the crisis administrator shall immediately retrieve the *documents from the head office building and deliver them to the corporate crisis centre'**. It may have been that the wording sounded like an order. Whatever the reason, the police officer in charge organised an escort to accompany the crisis administrator into the building to retrieve the documents.

Don't count on it working again – but, if you're desperate it's probably worth a try.

State of readiness

Finally, the strategy document should specify the state of readiness to be expected of the organisation. This will include the ongoing arrangements for maintaining the crisis management infrastructure, as well as the extent to which those arrangements, and the infrastructure itself, should be tested. These subjects are dealt with in some detail in later chapters.

The crisis management framework

In summary, the strategy document should present an overview of the framework for crisis management by addressing the following elements:

- What may be regarded as a corporate crisis.
- Where crisis leadership resides.
- Authorities and responsibilities during a crisis.
- Aims and objectives of crisis management.
- The point at which a crisis ends.
- Maintenance of the crisis management infrastructure.
- Testing the crisis management infrastructure.

Things you need to know...

**CRISIS MANAGEMENT STRATEGY
KEY QUESTIONS**

21 Is there a crisis management strategy document?

22 Has it been approved by the Board?

23 Have any crisis declaration trigger points been defined?

24 Is there a formal crisis management maintenance function in place?

25 Have the aims and objectives of the crisis management function been defined?

26 Do we have contacts with the emergency services?

27 How ready are we to deal with a crisis?

28 What are the crisis management testing arrangements?

THOROGOOD
PROFESSIONAL
INSIGHTS

Chapter 3

Command and control

Command and control

> **'Command and control'** is the most important element of managing a crisis, bar none. If you do nothing else, make sure you have in place a team capable of fulfilling this role.

Crisis management team

Every organisation should have a designated Crisis Management Team whose sole responsibility is to oversee completion of the crisis management mission, as described in Chapter 2.

As a team, it has nothing to do with maintenance of the crisis management infrastructure – it simply turns up 'on the night', does its job and goes away again – just like a cabaret artiste or a turn at a working men's club.

The team's job is to manage resolution of a crisis and it needs unfettered authority to do this. It should be able to call upon anybody within the organisation to assist and commit the organisation as it sees fit in order to achieve its overall objective.

Team make-up

The Crisis Management Team should be made up of members able to cover every aspect of the business (at high level). Each member will be chosen because of his or her knowledge and experience of a certain aspect of the business and will effectively be the team's expert when that aspect is considered. Should it become necessary to get down to minute detail, the member will know exactly who to contact for clarification and will have the ability to make that contact (see Chapter 4 on Communications).

The team needs to be compact in size. It must have adequate members to cover the business, as discussed in the previous paragraph, and to allow focused discussion; but it must not be so large that discussions become rambling and ineffective (the 'talking shop' syndrome). In my view, the optimum size for an effective crisis management team is four. A group of this size can quickly bond into a unit where each member knows and respects his or her colleagues and values their opinions. It may appear that, in a large organisation, four team members would not be able to cover every aspect of the business, so perhaps we need to re-define that requirement. In crisis management terms, it should be possible to distil the business down to four main areas:

- Customer services

- Operations

- Administration

- Technology

If you can categorise each aspect of your business under one of these four headings and can find four senior people, each able to represent one of them, you may have found your crisis management team. I say 'may' because it is important not to forget that these people have to be able to work together under extreme pressure – they must 'gel' as a team of equals, which means, amongst other things, that they must respect each other.

Deputies

There is a practical reason why you should keep the size of the crisis management team as low as possible. Each member needs to have at least one nominated deputy to take his or her place, if they are not available.

> *It's amazing how often a crisis strikes just at the time when all the members of the first team are off somewhere doing their own thing.*

If you can afford the luxury, I would recommend two deputies, although this is where you may experience some difficulty. You are likely to find, fairly quickly, that your organisation has a finite resource when it comes to people of the required calibre. This will be exacerbated when you start to build your subsidiary crisis teams (see Chapter 6 on Action teams/plans). Clearly, the larger the crisis management team, the more deputies you need to nominate, so, the best advice I can give is to keep it compact.

Reserves

Some organisations may feel the need to have an 'A' team and a 'B' team, the logic being that if you have a major crisis, the crisis management team is likely to be in session for a number of days. Given the pressure that the team would be under, they should not be expected to work for longer than eight to twelve hours at any time. This is not only a humane approach to the problem, it acknowledges that, over a period of time the team's judgement would be degraded – it would therefore be in the interests of the organisation to draft in fresh minds at the appropriate time. Whilst the logic is sound, setting up a second team presents a number of complications and adds to the overall expense and bureaucracy of the operation. It would seem a sensible compromise to form the first-named deputies into a 'B' team, as they will need training to the same level as the 'A' team members, in any event. In my view, any 'B' team taking over from the 'A' team during a crisis should do so purely as caretakers while the 'A' team is rested – there are significant complications in passing full control in such a situation.

Leadership

As with every aspect of life, the crisis management team needs a clear leader – somebody whose command will not be questioned and who will take full responsibility for his or her actions.

- What sort of person do we need for this critical role?
- What are the most important attributes of a crisis leader?
- How can we select the right person?

The most natural presumption (and in some situations, the safest) is that the leader of the crisis management team should be the top executive in the organisation – the Chief Operating Officer, Chief Executive or Managing Director – whatever the title.

This may not necessarily be the correct approach, though. Generally speaking, chief executives are famous for their autocratic style and their ability to make quick decisions. They are skilled at getting their own way in meetings – giants among the mere mortals that they manage. These are not the qualities that will get the best results from a crisis management team that is operating under extreme pressure.

The leader of a crisis management team needs to make full use of the technical and organisational skills available to him within his team – he cannot be an expert in every part of the business. He must listen to the advice given by his team-members, discuss the pros and cons and reach a consensus before committing to a course of action. Obviously, there may be moments, during the early stages of a crisis, when emergency decisions need to be made quickly, but these are likely to be rare. For the most part, the leader must project himself to his team-members as an equal who just happens to have the final say and who will take responsibility for the team in the final reckoning.

I came across a business resumption plan, a few years ago, where the crisis management team was headed up by a Chairman. The word 'chairman' is exactly right, in terms of the role required of the incumbent – but I didn't like it. For me, the word had connotations of long, leisurely meetings, minutes and a lack of action. My recommendation was that the title should be changed to 'Leader'. I gave my reasons and the recommendation was accepted. The role didn't change, but I like to think that everyone's perception of it did.

Invocation procedures

Now we will discuss the problem of invoking crisis procedures and, in particular, activation of the crisis management team.

When a crisis strikes, time will be of the essence.

It is imperative that your organisation has a procedure that will put the crisis management team in place (and in control) in the shortest possible time. In this context, there are a number of things to consider.

How the crisis manifests itself

In many cases, the crisis will present itself in physical form: a fire, a flood, an explosion, an impact, the breakdown of equipment or processes – we could probably go on. Will it be recognised as a crisis? After all, it may not start as a crisis – just a problem that could escalate. Will the possibility of escalation be recognised? By and large, you are in the hands of the people at the scene and reliant upon their awareness and their knowledge of the correct procedures.

When the crisis occurs

If the crisis occurs during working hours, it is possible that a member of staff will be among the first to become aware of it. In this scenario, the normal line reporting procedures should 'kick in' and the message should quickly reach an executive senior enough to take the correct action.

If the crisis occurs outside working hours, it is likely to be a security guard, or key holder (via the emergency services) who first becomes aware of any physical problem.

Of course, the 'non-physical' type of crisis might start with an unhelpful rumour, leading to an uncomplimentary TV news report, or the unwelcome attentions of a national newspaper reporter. In such a case you would be reliant upon a senior executive becoming aware and taking the correct action.

The mechanism for passing crisis information

In the final analysis, the decision on whether or not to invoke crisis procedures should rest with one person – the leader of the crisis management team. So, we need to have in place a mechanism for getting concise information to the leader quickly. We know, from previous paragraphs, that the information could come from a number of sources: security guards, key holders, executives, emergency services who cannot raise a key holder or even worried staff members who cannot contact a senior manager. We also know that it could come at any time of the day or night (24/7/365).

The mechanism needs to be robust, reliable and professional.

I would advocate the use of a call-handling company – one that will provide continuous service (again, 24/7/365) together with a unique telephone number, dedicated to your organisation's crisis invocation procedures.

Every member of your staff (including security guards and key holders) and the emergency services need to have the unique telephone number available at all times. As far as staff members are concerned, the number can be printed on their identity cards, but they must receive regular reminders on how and when to use it. The identity card is a good place to record the number for most organisations, as staff are required to carry it with them at all times whilst at work, so there is less chance of it going missing. In the case of the emergency services, the police would normally be involved in a crisis situation and it may therefore be helpful to negotiate with the local force to hold the crisis number as well as the normal key holder numbers.

Call-handling companies provide a number of services and it is therefore important that you make sure that your chosen company is prepared to provide the tailored service you need. The following points may prove helpful in any negotiations:

- Can the call company provide continuous cover (24/7/365)?

- Is the dedicated telephone number guaranteed for a period of time?

- Will the call company use an agreed script to handle incoming calls?

- Will the call company maintain contact lists to your instructions?

- Will the call company make calls in the stipulated sequence and timescales?

The first of the above points is self-evident. The ongoing availability of the dedicated telephone number may not be critical and there can be little doubt that telephone number changes will be forced on everyone, from time to time. It is, however, an expensive and time-consuming nuisance to have to keep re-issuing staff identity cards, so it's worth getting what comfort you can on this point.

It is important that the call company uses an agreed script for incoming calls. You may be excused for thinking that this will help them screen out any time-wasting calls, but this is not recommended, in case a wrong decision is made. What it will do is to help ensure that the crisis management team leader, to whom the message will be passed, receives pertinent information.

The following example script should be considered:

1   Hello, this is the (your organisation's name) crisis line.

2   What is your name? (Repeat back for confirmation)

3   What is your role? (E.g., Manager, XYZ Dept/Key Holder) (Repeat back for confirmation)

4   (For members of staff) Who is your immediate manager? (Repeat back for confirmation)

5   Where are you? (Repeat back for confirmation)

6   Why are you calling? (Repeat back for confirmation, get exact info)

7   Is there any danger to you or anyone else? (If appropriate)

8   Are the emergency services aware? (If appropriate)

9   Do you require me to call the emergency services?(If appropriate)

10 Please give a telephone number you can be reached on. (Repeat back for confirmation)

11   Thank you for calling the (your organisation's name) crisis line.

12   The details will be passed on to the appropriate person and you will be contacted in due course.

13   This call is timed at (current local time).

14   End call.

Once the call company is in receipt of a crisis call (and has called the emergency services, if necessary), it must immediately set in motion its crisis notification procedures, using the prescribed contact lists, which are, hopefully, up-to-date. The lists will identify the crisis management team leader and his deputy, or deputies, and the calls should be made in the designated sequence.

Code-words

It may be sufficient that the call company simply telephones the appropriate person and repeats the message, as received. This has the benefit of being direct and saving time, so long as the person can be reached by telephone (home, office, car, mobile).

If more security is required, a crisis code-word can be used before delivering the message – a secure code-word issued by an appropriate person in your organisation and known only to the crisis management team members and the call company. This will prevent bogus calls as well as ensuring a healthy adrenaline flow on the part of the crisis team leader when he hears the code-word.

Security can be further improved by the use of pagers instead of telephones. If a pager is issued to the leader and his deputies, the call company will be able to send the code-word to the pager and wait for a callback from the leader, when full details will be given. It is an added benefit of such a system that, if the leader is away on holiday, or otherwise indisposed, he can pass his pager on to his deputy, thus speeding up the contact times. The call company would be required to call other pagers after a certain time, if no call back is received. The call company would also have telephone numbers to fall back on.

How a crisis is declared

Now let us look at the procedures that the crisis team leader needs to follow when details of a possible crisis are received. It doesn't matter whether he has received these details direct or has called the company back to obtain them, following receipt of a paged code-word.

We need to understand that the leader could be anywhere, or doing anything when the call is made. The procedures need to make allowance for this and he needs to be provided not only with a pager (if that is the chosen route) but also enough telephone facilities to ensure that he is contactable, and able to make contact, at all times.

It is important that the leader documents the information received, together with the time of receipt. He should have a ready supply of the form designed for this purpose; we shall call it the 'Crisis Declaration Log' because it will be used to record the leader's decision on whether or not to declare a crisis, together with the action taken at the time.

So, let us suppose that the crisis management team leader has received details of a report from the call company and has recorded them, as received, on his Crisis Declaration Log. He now has to assimilate the information and decide whether or not to declare a crisis.

If he decides that the event does **not** warrant a declaration, he will advise the call company that this is the case and instruct them to 'stand down'. This might happen in the majority of cases where, with the best of intentions, people report minor problems as a crisis. There may be a need for the leader to contact an appropriate manager to investigate and report back to him, but that is his call.

If, on the other hand, the leader decides to declare a crisis, what should happen next?

Activating the crisis management team

The first thing will have been to advise the call company that a crisis has been declared and to record the timing of this. The next step depends upon the chosen route for communicating with other members of the team. There are a number of options:

- **The leader calls other team members personally** – not recommended – he will have enough on his plate.

- **The leader calls a specified member of staff, whose job it is to raise the team** – a better option, but still reliant on contact being made.

- **The leader activates dedicated software that automatically makes the necessary calls** – a good, modern option – so long as the software is proven, always accessible and, most importantly, properly maintained.

- **The leader uses the call company to make the necessary contacts** – an elegant solution as he is already in contact with the company.

I believe that the final option is the most effective, because it removes the need for the leader to think about anything other than the team members he needs with him. Apart from that, his mind should be solely fixed on getting to the crisis management rendezvous and setting up his 'command post' as quickly as possible. What he shouldn't have to do is explain what has happened repeatedly to everyone he contacts.

> *I do not dismiss the dedicated software option – at the end of the day it comes down to what you feel most comfortable with and I am aware that there are some excellent products available.*

Let us proceed on the basis that the call company's arrangements extend to raising the crisis management team.

1   Once the leader has advised the call company that he is declaring a crisis, he will instruct them to contact each member of the team.

2   The call company will have standing orders to move on to the appropriate deputies if contact is not made within a certain timescale.

3   The call company will have standing orders to report progress once an agreed time period has elapsed and to carry out further instructions until told to stand down.

4   The leader is now free to make his way to the crisis meeting point.

Some while ago, I organised an acid test (see Chapter 8) of the crisis management team for an organisation I worked for. The activation mechanisms were as discussed above and the test resulted in a number of amendments to standing procedures.

At about 7.00a.m. one Monday morning, each member of the team received a call from the call company advising them that a landslip had occurred adjacent to the building that housed the mainframe computer system (this building was on a steep hill next to a major construction site on which huge excavations were in progress – the scenario was credible). The effect of the landslip had been to partially demolish the building, destroying the computer installation. In addition, the operations staff members on duty at the time were not accounted for.

The team members were advised that the leader had declared a crisis and they were to make their way to the crisis team meeting point as soon as possible.

I was disappointed with the amount of time it took some team members to arrive at the meeting point and noted, furthermore, that they did not seem particularly stressed – which they should have been given that it was meant to be an acid test.

The reason was simple: They had all received information about the nature of the crisis, one or two of them had taken time out to telephone the computer installation and had established that nothing had happened. It then took them a little while to conclude that it was not a hoax and, after conferring with each other, they decided that they should go to the meeting point anyway. The surprise element of the test was ruined, but it continued and a number of issues were raised which enabled us to improve our processes further (**no test is a failure – there are always lessons to learn**).

The main lessons learned in relation to activating the crisis management team on this occasion were as follows:

1   Precede any crisis callout message with a prearranged code-word

2   Do not give details of the crisis to team members when contacting them. It takes up precious time and could lead to a protracted question and answer session

3   Restrict the message to: '(code-word) a crisis has been declared by (leader's name). Please go to (the prearranged meeting point) immediately where you will receive full details.' (Agree script with call company.)

4   Provide each team member (and deputy) with a 'Crisis Pack' which contains a location map of the prearranged meeting point and instructions on initial duties should a crisis be declared. Such instructions should include an order NOT to question crisis callout messages that are preceded by the correct code-word

Having arrived at the point where we can successfully activate our crisis management team, we now need to consider where they will operate from and what facilities they will need.

The crisis centre

If feasible, the best solution is a dedicated crisis management facility – the Crisis Centre.

Such a facility needs to be located well away from the main premises of the organisation, so as to avoid it becoming unavailable as a result of any crisis involving denial of access to those premises.

The existence and/or location of the centre will not be publicised. Its usefulness will be compromised if it becomes a centre of media attention when activated.

Team members (and deputies) need to know how to get to the Crisis Centre and how to gain access to it (see 'Crisis Pack' above).

The centre needs to be self-contained and have the following facilities:

- A private meeting room in which the team will operate.
- An adjoining room in which support staff will operate.
- Television and video facilities.
- Radio and cassette recorder facilities.
- Dedicated telephone lines with answerphone facilities.
- A cell phone.
- Fax machines (ideally two – one to receive, one to send).
- A photocopier.
- A personal computer/laptop, with printer and modem (not networked).
- Stationery supplies (including whiteboard).
- Emergency data and information (contact lists, organisation charts, etc).

- Catering facilities.

- Toilet facilities.

- Standby power facilities.

Crisis support staff

Mention is made, in the above list, of an adjoining room for support staff. This may seem like an unnecessary luxury, but I have seen crisis management team members totally tied up answering telephones, recording radio newsflashes and reading faxes. If this happens, the turmoil caused in the team room destroys the ability for reasoned discussion and means that one or more members will be excluded for significant periods of time.

If the support staff option is accepted, the support team members will have to be trained in much the same way as the crisis management team and they will have to be included in the callout arrangements.

It is advisable that one of the support team members should be the key holder for the crisis centre, living fairly close to the site, as is the norm with key holders. This should remove the need for crisis management team members to have to gain access to the centre (although they should be able to, if necessary). Other members will need secretarial skills.

Crisis Support Staff will have the following duties:

- Open the crisis centre and prepare for the arrival of the crisis management team.

- Deal with all communications into the centre, pass messages on to the team.

- Service the team, run errands, arrange meetings, take notes, provide refreshments.

- Maintain the security of the centre – exclude unauthorised personnel.

At this point we have a properly declared crisis and an empowered crisis management team in a viable crisis centre with appropriate facilities and support staff.

Now what?

Now they are going to manage the crisis.

Managing the crisis

Managing a crisis is more of an art than a science, with the crisis management team having to 'go with the flow', or even 'roll with the punches', as events unfold before them. Having said that, there should be a structure, which the leader should seek to apply, in order to ensure that time is not wasted in pontificating on the likely effects of events that may not happen, or discussing events which have already happened and cannot be changed.

The team leader should be provided with a checklist, which the team can loosely work through, depending on the nature of the crisis (it makes sense for the support staff to have this ready at the crisis centre for when the team arrives).

The summarised version of a typical checklist is given in Appendix 1.

Documentation

Earlier in this chapter, I gave my views on the role of the crisis management support staff and these included 'taking notes'. Earlier still, I expressed my dislike of the term 'chairman' to describe the crisis management team leader, citing the 'long meetings/ minute taking' mentality that the name implied.

An apparent contradiction?

No. The fact is that, for many organisations, it will be absolutely essential that a post mortem be carried out, once normal service is resumed. This will serve a number of purposes, from helping to improve procedures and instructions for the future, to justifying the decisions of the crisis team at the time they were made. I have always advocated the maintenance of a **'Crisis Log'**, which shows the key milestones and the times that they occurred.

What you **do not need** is a long-hand, blow-by-blow account of everything done or every word said in the room. That sort of 'tour de force' would never see the light of day and it would serve no useful purpose.

The crisis log

Use members of the support staff to keep the crisis log, and rotate them from time to time – it's a stressful job. It's also a job that requires specific training to ensure that the final log is fit for its purpose. To this end, make sure that the people chosen can write legibly!

Use pro-forma, pre-numbered, hard copy log sheets or a specific word processing format, if you have stand-alone computer facilities. In considering which medium to use, take into account the possibility that the crisis could involve loss of power or network connections and always have hard copy format to fall back on.

I prefer hard copy log sheets and would advocate that a member of the crisis management team should check and initial each sheet as it is completed. This may seem unnecessarily bureaucratic, but the log is the team's proof of the rationale behind its decisions and it is important that it is verified contemporaneously.

Give 'crisis log scribes' a standard system to work to, such as the word **'IDEA'**, which, in this context, stands for: **Information, Decisions, Events and Actions**. The instruction being that only these elements should be recorded in the log.

Taking the above approach, an example of a typical crisis log is given in Appendix 2.

The amount of discussion that will have taken place between each of the events recorded in the example log will have been significant – but that is not important to being able to follow the thrust of the team's work. It goes without saying that the 'scribe' should stay well in the background and not assume the position of an extra crisis management team member. There may be times, however, when he or she may have to ask for clarification, particularly where the discussion takes a technical turn or a decision is left hanging (this can happen where team members know each other so well that they do not need to 'spell things out').

Command and control summary

In this chapter we have covered the following aspects of command and control:

- Constitution and make-up of the crisis management team.

- Requirements of the crisis management team leader.

- Crisis invocation procedures.

- The mechanism for passing crisis information.

- Declaring a crisis.

- Activating the crisis management team.

- The crisis centre.

- Crisis support staff.

- Managing the crisis.

- Crisis management documentation – the crisis log.

Things you need to know...

CRISIS COMMAND AND CONTROL KEY QUESTIONS

29 Is there a designated crisis management team?

30 What are the team's aims and objectives?

31 Are these aims and objectives properly documented and periodically reviewed?

32 Who is the leader?

33 Are there designated deputies?

34 What is the procedure for crisis notification?

35 How is the team activated?

36 Where will the team operate from?

37 What facilities are made available to the team?

38 What guidance is there for managing a crisis?

39 What arrangements exist for documenting a crisis?

Chapter 4

Communications

Chapter 4
Communications

In the previous chapter, we touched on the need for a robust communications network in three separate areas concerned with command and control of a crisis:

- Crisis notification (the initial alarm call).

- Activating the crisis management team.

- Managing the crisis.

In this chapter, we will explore these in more depth, looking at some of the problems and pitfalls, and ensuring that the final arrangements are satisfactory. We will then discuss the need for communications channels in other areas of the crisis management function.

Crisis notification

We have concluded that notification of a physical crisis event can come from a number of sources:

- Staff members (during or outside working hours).

- Security staff and/or key holders (outside working hours).

- The emergency services (normally police – outside working hours).

We have direct control over the first two sources and can negotiate assistance with the third.

The first two sources will carry a unique crisis notification telephone number as part of their staff identity cards, which means they should always have access to it. If, as is the case for many organisations, the security guards (or key holders) are provided by an external supplier, it will be necessary to make alternative arrangements, such as including the telephone number at the top of the schedule of contact numbers that they have access to whilst on duty.

Staff awareness

Turning to the provision of the crisis notification telephone number to members of staff, it will be necessary to make sure that they are aware, and are kept aware, of what is expected of them. The periodic issue of a general staff notice, say every six months, should achieve this.

It is important that these periodic notices are not simply the same message, reproduced every six months. The document will have more impact if it includes interesting anecdotes, perhaps praising actions recently taken by staff members who have followed the instructions, or even reporting crises in other organisations and making positive comments about the arrangements in place in this organisation – anything (in context) to gain and keep the recipients' attention.

Remember to ensure that new members of staff receive crisis information as part of their induction packs.

Consider reinforcing the message (very occasionally) at staff briefing sessions.

Returning to the periodic general notice, the following bullet points show the kind of information that might be included:

- The ongoing viability of the organisation is in everyone's interests: Customers, management and staff. We must work together to ensure that we are able to counter any threats to our continued progress.

- Your staff identity card, which you must carry with you at all times during working hours, has the organisation's crisis notification telephone number printed on it (give number).

- There are certain, rare circumstances when you must use this number, as specified below.

- If you become aware of a serious threat to the organisation's operations (a possible crisis), report it immediately to any manager.

- If you are unable to contact a manager, and are concerned for the safety of members of the public, members of staff or disruption to the organisation's operations, get to a telephone and dial the crisis notification number immediately (if necessary, call the emergency services first).

- On connection to the crisis notification number you will be asked the following questions:
    - Your name
    - Your position
    - Your immediate manager

- Your location

- The problem

- If anyone is in danger

- If the emergency services need calling

- The number you can be called back on.

- Keep your answers brief and to the point. You will be thanked, told the time of the message and advised that the information will be passed to the appropriate person and that you will be contacted in due course.

- Do not allow access to the crisis notification telephone number to persons not employed by the organisation.

- Do not be afraid to use the number if you witness threatening situations, as specified above, or have them reported to you by a reliable source. It is better to be safe than sorry.

- Wanton or frivolous use of the number will lead to disciplinary proceedings.

(N.B. There are conflicting messages in the final two bullet points above – it is important to achieve the right balance here and throughout the notice.)

Later in this chapter, we will look at other messages that we need to pass on to members of staff. Think carefully before amalgamating them all into one message.

So many people carry personal mobile phones these days that we tend to forget that some members of staff may have to find a public telephone box, and have the necessary small change, to make the call. Consideration should, perhaps, be given to making the crisis notification number free of charge.

Assessing crisis notification calls

In the previous chapter, the benefits of using a call handling company were discussed and it was concluded that the company would need an agreed script to deal with crisis notification calls.

It is inevitable that the company will receive inappropriate calls from time to time and we touched on the inadvisability of allowing the company to decide whether or not these calls should be passed on. Certainly, most call companies would not be prepared to make such a judgment, unless their actions were fully indemnified by the client, fearing repercussions should they make the wrong decision.

In my opinion, it is safer that all calls be passed on for action.

Unless you fear for the health or sanity of your crisis management team leader (the nominated receiver of crisis calls), it's best to accept that inappropriate calls will be received and take comfort from the fact that each call represents a test of the crisis notification mechanism.

A few years ago, my organisation experienced a spate of lost identity cards. In one case, a member of the public found a card in a public house on a Sunday evening and dutifully telephoned the crisis notification number to report the matter. The call company logged the call and alerted the crisis management team leader by paging the crisis code-word to him. On calling the company back, he decided against declaring a crisis. I found out, fairly early on the Monday morning that the call had ruined the end of his weekend and the inevitable request was received to improve the system to ensure that future false alarms would be screened out.

It is a simple matter to instruct the call company to deal with reports of found cards quite separately from all other calls, but I concluded that no other dispensation was possible. It was, in my opinion, far too dangerous to allow the call company to exercise its judgment, except in that one specific scenario, provision for which could be made in the standing instructions/scripts to which the company worked.

Lost cards are not a major problem, but it may be worth considering offering a small reward for their return. You may be lucky enough to be able to print this additional information on the card itself, thus reducing the incidence of call company involvement. In most cases, however, there will not be enough room for additional wording and it will have to be left to the call company to deal with the matter. Callers should simply be requested to return the card, together with their name and address, to the organisation's personnel department, who will send them a voucher or cheque by return.

It is possible that the reward scheme could be financed by a charge levied on staff each time they lose their identity card. If you are able to impose such a charge, it should focus minds and reduce the number of losses significantly.

Summarising our discussions on crisis notification communications, we have concluded the following:

- That staff need to be made, and kept, aware of what is required of them.

- That the call company (or other medium chosen to handle crisis notification calls) needs to be provided with very specific instructions and scripts to ensure that there is no deviation from the required line.

Activating the crisis management team

The next stage in the process involves activation of the crisis management team and we have already concluded, in the previous chapter, that it makes sense to use the call company for this purpose. To recapitulate, the main reason for this is that the crisis management team leader needs to concentrate on getting to his 'command post' and thinking about how to approach the crisis, rather than diverting his attention to the subject of contacting his crisis team colleagues.

We touched upon the fact that software is available that can be programmed to make the necessary calls in the right order, move on to alternative numbers if there is no answer and report back on progress. Some organisations may consider this to be a perfectly acceptable solution, but, for myself, when the stakes are as high as they can be in a crisis situation, I would much rather rely upon a human interface than an electronic one.

In the interests of fairness, I do acknowledge that advances are being made all the time in the technology field and I would recommend that you investigate the current software available before closing your mind to this option.

Contacting the team leader

Whatever methodology is chosen, one thing remains essential: The team leader must be contacted with the minimum of delay. There must be a set sequence for calling the appropriate people, which is subject to strict time constraints. Figure 2 shows the sort of routine that might be followed by a call company in order to contact the team leader. Notice how more time is initially given to contacting the designated team leader himself, before moving on to his deputies. This is quite normal because the leader is, by definition, the person that you would most want to lead your team – that's why he was chosen. However good the deputies are, they are still the second and third choices, respectively. Having said that, you cannot hang on for him indefinitely, and the process provides for a fairly swift progression through the various options.

In an organisation with well-defined and well-maintained crisis procedures, it would be most unlikely that the call company would get beyond the first step: calling the team leader's designated pager. There are two main reasons for this:

- The team leader would be fully aware of his responsibilities and would always have his pager switched on and accessible.

- If the team leader were unavailable at any time (away on holiday or indisposed through illness) he would have physically passed his pager on to his first deputy.

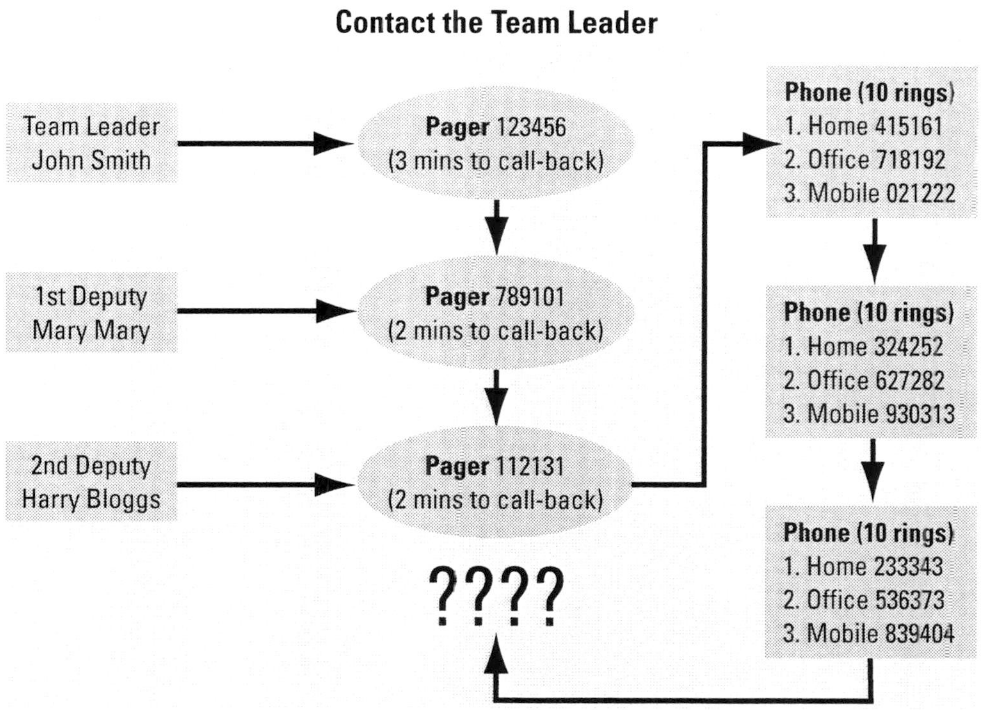

Contact the Team Leader

Figure 2: A pre-planned calling sequence with deadlines is essential

Obviously, if the leader were to be unavailable for a protracted period, some consideration would have to be given to appointing another deputy and amending the contact list(s) for the duration.

Fallback arrangements

It is almost inconceivable that the call company would have failed to reach somebody before it had exhausted all of the possibilities shown in Figure 2. Having said that, the fact that these procedures are meant to cover crisis situations means that we should have in place some form of fallback instruction. The initial requirement might be to start again with the leader's pager number, but there has to be an overall time constraint. It might be considered reasonable to stipulate that the call company should also hold the relevant address details of the people involved (we are only talking about the leader and his deputies, here) and, if no contact has been made after (say) an hour, then the police should be asked to help trace the individuals concerned.

It should be emphasised that the above is a worst-case scenario, which would only occur if the organisation did not take its crisis management procedures seriously or the designated officers did not act responsibly.

Contacting the rest of the crisis management team and support staff

Clearly, the critical thing is to contact a leader. Once he/she is in place, the crisis management process has started – if the worst comes to the worst, the leader could get to the crisis centre and then set about contacting team members and support staff personally – this could happen, to some extent, if the call company were ultimately unsuccessful in reaching everyone they had been instructed to contact. The trouble is, any delay at the start of a crisis can be expensive. It therefore makes sense, as discussed in earlier paragraphs, for the leader to delegate this duty to the call company.

So, assuming the crisis centre is to be used, what will the leader require?

- The support team to get to the crisis centre immediately.

- Other crisis management team members to get to the crisis centre immediately.

- Specific action team leaders to be put on notice (perhaps).

The call company will therefore need individual call routines, similar to those shown in Figure 2, for the following people:

- The leader of the support team, and deputy or deputies.

- Each crisis management team member, and deputy or deputies.

- Each action team leader, and deputy or deputies.

As was mentioned earlier, whilst the fulfilment of these contacts is important, it is not as critical as making the first contact with the crisis management team leader. Thus, it is not essential to have the same kind of fallback arrangements; it will not be necessary to extend the information held by the call company to private addresses.

The standing instructions are likely to be that the call company should telephone the crisis centre every (say) 20 minutes (initially, perhaps, leaving an answerphone message) to give an update on its success in reaching people and/or to seek further instructions.

Once the leader is satisfied with the contacts made, he will instruct the call company to 'stand down' and, if necessary, instruct the support staff, or fellow team members, to attempt to contact any stragglers.

From the above, it will be evident that a significant amount of up-to-date information needs to be retained at a number of different locations:

- The call company.

- The crisis management team leader and deputies.

- The crisis centre.

The information also needs to held by the organisation centrally, in case the nature of the crisis dictates that it is better managed from the familiar surroundings of the crisis team leader's day-to-day office accommodation (not advisable unless the benefits are significant).

What must be stressed is that the communications information referred to above is absolutely useless unless it is kept totally up-to-date. The procedures and routines necessary to achieve this are discussed in Chapter 7.

Managing the crisis

Once the team leader, his crisis management team and support staff members are assembled at the crisis centre, the need for trouble free communications is absolutely essential. Without it, the crisis will simply not be managed.

In Chapter 3 on Command and control, we discussed the facilities that the crisis management team needed at the crisis centre and the extent to which the support staff would assist in managing communications in and out of the centre. This management is essential to the crisis management team's well being, because the amount of traffic in the early stages of a crisis could well swamp them, if there were no 'buffer'.

We now understand the need for extensive communications equipment at the crisis centre, together with the need to ensure that it is always ready to be used at a moment's notice. We also understand the need to ensure that up-to-date principal contact lists are available at the crisis centre.

Now let's look at the subsidiary communications requirements for effective crisis management.

The public relations team

In Chapter 3 on Command and control we saw how the crisis management team would need to make early contact with the public relations team leader to establish that the PR team were considering the implications of the crisis and that they were preparing a media-handling plan. The details of the latter will be covered in Chapter 5.

It is clear that the PR team would need access to various communications channels in order to do their job properly – the PR action plan would therefore need to make provision for a base which would be equipped with the appropriate facilities, in much the same way as the crisis centre itself. If you have large enough premises, you could consider housing a number of action teams in the same building as the crisis management team, so long as they were all separately accommodated (NB: NOT in, or close to, your main business accommodation!).

The PR team would need to be able to communicate with:

- **The crisis management team** – to give and receive information and agree policy.

- **The emergency services** – to receive up-to-date information on the crisis (damage, casualties, etc).

- **The human resources team** – to pass on and agree the way in which staff, or their relatives are to be contacted.

- **The organisation's media representative** – to brief on the 'official line' and to organise interviews.

- **The media** – to issue statements and arrange press conferences/interviews.

- **Customer-facing branches/outlets** – to issue a common corporate message and provide scripted official responses to queries from customers.

- **The organisation's normal business call centre** – to provide scripted official responses to telephone callers.

The need for up-to-date contact lists for all of the above is obvious. The PR team will also need a bulk fax facility, stationery supplies and, if possible, e-mail facilities. In either case, pre-organised mailing lists that can be activated at a stroke are essential.

The human resources team

In Chapter 3 on Command and control, we saw how the crisis management team needed to contact the HR team leader fairly early on to establish the personnel implications of the crisis and to deal with the treatment of any casualty situations.

The HR team would need similar facilities to the PR team, as discussed in the immediately preceding paragraphs.

The HR team would need to be able to communicate with:

- **The crisis management team** – to give and receive information and agree policy.

- **Local hospitals** – to receive up-to-date information on casualties, etc.

- **The emergency services** – to provide personal details of casualties (next of kin, etc).

- **The public relations team** – to agree the way in which staff, or their relatives are to be contacted.

- **The relatives of staff casualties** – to provide assistance and support (after notification – which would be a matter for the emergency services).

- **Specific members of staff with alternative skills** – HR should have a register of members of staff able to perform other, key roles in the organisation.

- **General and specific employment agencies** – to obtain replacement members of staff, if necessary.

- **The staff, as a whole** – to issue updates on the crisis, forbid media comment and give instructions on attendance, or otherwise, for work.

As in the case of the PR team, numerous detailed and up-to-date contact lists need to be maintained, particularly in the case of the next of kin of members of staff, where extreme sensitivity is required. Naturally, all HR departments will have this information in their staff files, but they need to have access to a copy at their crisis base – one that is as up-to-date as the main files.

Contacting relatives of injured members of staff in order to provide help and support is a task requiring a great deal of tact and diplomacy, which must be handled on an individual basis. This is not the case in relation to general messages to staff members. These can be handled by way of a communications cascade.

Communications cascades

The communications cascade is a relatively simple and effective means of communicating messages to a large and disparate number of people within an organisation.

In the context of crisis management, it relies upon the maintenance of an infrastructure whereby each member of staff carries the home telephone numbers of:

- Their immediate superior.

- Their immediate subordinates, or direct reports.

Staff members who do not have other members of staff reporting directly to them should therefore need to have one telephone number only – that of their immediate manager; whilst managers should have one telephone number for their immediate superior and a telephone number for each direct report.

The only complexity occurs when a staff member is also a member of the crisis management team – in which case, he or she should be excluded from the cascade, for obvious reasons.

Once this infrastructure is established, it should be possible to set up a communications cascade very quickly by issuing a general instruction. As with other contact lists, the main problem will be ensuring that the various telephone numbers are kept up-to-date. If you are lucky enough to have some form of control certification process in your organisation, the maintenance of the communications cascade should be one of the controls that each manager is required to certify as being in place.

The HR team would employ the communications cascade by issuing the necessary messages to line executives (at as high a level as is possible). The information would then ripple down the cascade without HR having to remain involved.

It may be that different messages would need to be cascaded to different sections of the staff:

- Some staff may be asked to stay at home until further notice.

- Some staff may be asked to report for duty as usual.

- Some staff may be asked to report to a different location until further notice.

- Staff in non-essential departments may be asked to report to managers of essential departments to help out.

One thing that's worth remembering is that, if the crisis occurs just before a payday, some staff will be more concerned about whether or not they are going to be paid than where or when they are going to work – it's human nature, so remember to cover that eventuality in your HR planning!

It's also worth remembering that members of staff who are working through a crisis, perhaps in uncomfortable temporary accommodation, will be subject to increased stresses. It may cause specific problems, for instance, to young parents who may have to travel further to work and work longer hours. As well as the resolution of their practical difficulties, these people need continuous reassurance and this will become a major communications exercise for the HR team as the crisis proceeds.

The PR team may well reinforce the communications cascade by issuing a telephone number to the HR team that staff can call to get a standard message about the crisis. This is fine, so long as the message is fairly optimistic in tone and short on specific details. The detailed information needs to be passed down the cascade itself to avoid unwanted disclosures to outside parties.

I have seen plans that included this staff information telephone number being given out on local radio, which is an invitation to all and sundry to find out what is really happening.

Communications summary

In this chapter, we have covered the following aspects of communications in a crisis:

- Crisis notification.
- Staff awareness.
- Assessing crisis notification calls.
- Activating the crisis management team.
- Contacting the crisis management team leader.
- Fallback arrangements for contacting the team leader.
- Contacting the rest of the crisis management team and support staff.
- Managing the crisis.
- Requirements within the public relations team.
- Requirements within the human resources team.
- Communications cascades.

Things you need to know...

CRISIS COMMUNICATIONS
KEY QUESTIONS

40 What are the crisis notification arrangements?

41 What steps are taken to ensure ongoing staff awareness of arrangements?

42 How are crisis notification calls assessed?

43 What arrangements are there for contacting the crisis management team leader?

44 How is the rest of the crisis management team contacted?

45 What fallback arrangements exist to cover failure to make contact?

46 Are contact routines fully documented and kept up-to-date?

47 Where are copies of the contact routines kept?

48 Are the contact routines subject to regular audit?

49 What arrangements exist for handling communications in and out of the crisis centre?

50 What arrangements exist for public relations communications during a crisis?

51 What arrangements exist for human resources related communications during a crisis?

52 Is there a communications cascade system in place, if so, how does it work?

Chapter 5

Organising the media interface

Chapter 5
Organising the media interface

Media attention

If your business relies upon public confidence, either because the general public are prospective customers (food and beverages, fast moving consumer goods, etc), or because substantial numbers have their personal assets invested in your business (savers, shareholders, etc), you will have to devote resource to maintaining that confidence.

> *The more your company is in the public eye, the more attention you will get from the media.*

Reputational damage

Do not underestimate the reputational damage that can be caused to your business by the onset of a major crisis, or, more to the point, the way that crisis is handled.

A minor event, resulting in short-term business interruption, might only attract local newspaper reporters, but if there are casualties, it is a completely different 'ball-game', with possible interest from national television news and, if you are an international player, worldwide attention.

> The stakes are high – if the physical effects of the crisis don't get you, public relations errors could.

We know that the main objective of the public relations action team is to limit the reputational damage suffered by an organisation during, or as a result of, a corporate crisis. This objective acquires major significance in an organisation that is in the public eye. As indicated in the preceding paragraph, mishandled public relations can lead to a quite separate crisis, which could well dwarf the original crisis in terms of the adverse effect it could have on the business.

Sources of information

In drawing up its crisis action plan, the public relations function needs to consider the different sources of information available to the general public (via the media) on the subject of the crisis. Once the sources are identified, procedures for controlling or influencing them need to be put in place.

Let's look at some of the more obvious sources of media information:

- **The physical evidence of the crisis, including eye witnesses** – in this day and age, images of disaster scenes can be seen all over the world before a crisis management function is even in place. This is the starting point for public relations efforts – it is the 'given' – it cannot be controlled or influenced.

- **The emergency services** – media reporters will often seek to get on-site statements from emergency services representatives – normally only factual statements will be made about the extent of damage/ casualties, etc. The opportunity for control or influence is very limited, but it is highly unlikely that professionals will make statements criticising a business in such a situation. If such statements are made, however, a decision needs to be taken on whether to counter them immediately or remain silent. If there are casualties, the public relations team needs to react quickly to demonstrate the organisation's regret and compassion for those affected.

- **Staff members at the scene, possibly involved and in shock** – a potentially damaging information source – 'I've been telling them for years something like this would happen....' – It is likely to be impossible to stop the media getting to such people in the immediate aftermath of an event and general staff rules forbidding media statements will, understandably, be forgotten in the heat of the moment. The effect of adverse comments needs to be influenced by neutralising them, if at all possible – 'Mr X has gone through a great deal and our first thoughts are for his welfare. We are surprised by his comments – they will have to be thoroughly investigated once we've dealt with the immediate problem'.

- **Archive reports of similar crises suffered by your organisation** – keep your fingers crossed that there are none!

- **Staff members away from the scene** – it is possible that remote reporters will seek out local members of staff to interview them about the disaster and obtain their views on the effects on the business. This risk can be fully controlled, if the public relations team acts quickly enough. It is important to contact everybody as soon as the crisis breaks – the first instruction might simply be to say nothing to anybody until further notice – it can always be followed up, at the appropriate time, with the official line that certain managers may be permitted to pass on to the media. Clearly, if remote senior members of staff are set up to say certain things to the media, they should be 'fed' with updated information, as the crisis develops.

- **Public relations team output** – this is the only real PR weapon with which to support the organisation in managing the crisis. Reactive output, as discussed in previous bullet points, is fine, but the team needs to become proactive as quickly as possible – to take the initiative and give the media the messages that the organisation wants them to have. Press releases can be faxed to news agencies and other, direct media contacts and, if the situation demands it, the organisation's 'media front man' can be 'wheeled out' at a press conference to spell out the official line on the crisis.

The front man

Who is your 'front man', the public face of your organisation?

Generally speaking, I would expect you to interpret any references to the masculine gender in this report as also including the feminine gender. So, please do not consider the term 'front man' to be politically incorrect. The fact is it can be preferable to actually have a female 'front man' in some situations, particularly where the organisation wants to present to the public a warm, compassionate image. That may sound unduly devious (heaven forbid), but the fact is it happens all the time and you need to use every trick available to you to rescue your organisation from the crisis that threatens to destroy it.

Your front man may be your Chairman or Chief Executive Officer – always presuming that you have managed to keep him or her out of the crisis management team, as advocated in Chapter 3 on Command and control.

I have always thought that fronting the media offensive was the perfect job for a chief executive officer. Not only is it a very important job, requiring maturity, experience and stature; it also keeps him out of the way of the crisis management team. In some organisations, the strength of personality of the chief executive officer can make it extremely difficult for the crisis management team leader to assume the authority that is needed to manage the crisis properly – interference and second-guessing by the chief executive can seriously dent a crisis team's confidence. Much better that he should be kept busy doing a job that, arguably, only he can do properly.

Media training

Let's step back for a moment and see where we are. Has your preferred media front man had media training? If not, consider it, because this is the person that the national media would be allowed to interview, firstly on the crisis itself and secondly on the cause and effects of the crisis – you cannot afford 'loose cannons' at such a critical time.

Even if your front man has had years of experience, giving interviews and holding press conferences, media training could still be of benefit. The better the training the more chance that standards will be maintained and rules remembered when the pressure is on.

Basic rules (e.g. if you receive a telephone call from a reporter asking for information, never respond immediately – always ring them back) can be forgotten under pressure, sometimes with disastrous results.

The media fixer

Large organisations would benefit from a 'media fixer' – somebody who would be able to organise press releases and conferences – somebody who deals with the media regularly and has established relationships of trust, where possible.

It is likely that the media fixer will be the public relations team leader – in fact, that is probably one of the most important attributes that the leader will need.

It is vital to get the media onside as soon as possible and to start dictating the agenda in terms of proactive communication – this is where trust and established relationships will be particularly useful.

The aim is to dictate where, when and how the right messages will be given to the media.

The right messages

The most important messages that you would wish to get over would concern the containment of the crisis and the organisation's (undoubted) ability to overcome it with the minimum of disruption and inconvenience to customers. In fact, if you can say that customers will not suffer in any way, so much the better. Don't say it if it can be immediately disproved, however, as this would tend to exacerbate, rather than improve, the situation.

The focus of the messages you would seek to get across would be significantly different in a situation where there were serious casualties. In such a case, compassion for those affected and their loved ones needs to be shown before the effects on the business are discussed.

There is significant value in having pre-prepared scripts that can be quickly tailored to the specific circumstances of a crisis. Getting the right messages out without delay can create the impression of a management team totally in control and allay negative speculation.

There is, however, danger in going too fast. Events that are still unfolding could negate any 'good vibes' resulting from premature messages. Prior approval from the crisis management team will help avoid such problems.

An additional benefit of pre-prepared scripts, that cover a range of crisis situations, is that their very existence indicates that the public relations team has thought through a number of possibilities. Whether this has been as a result of scenario testing or 'near miss' situations is immaterial – what is important is that everything possible is done to reduce the need for original thinking during a high pressure crisis situation.

The official line

In an organisation with a number of customer-facing outlets, those outlets need to be instructed very quickly on the official line. This was touched on in a preceding paragraph, in relation to remote staff and media contacts. Here, though, we are concerned about the effect that rumours spread by worried customers can have on an organisation.

There's nothing worse than an employee telling a customer that they have no idea what is going on (nobody tells us anything, etc). Not only does this give the impression to the customer of an organisation with no leadership, it is also another route whereby the media might be able to create a story along those lines. In the worst-case scenario, the 'customer' could be a newspaper reporter looking for such a story. As before, if you are not ready to issue definitive instructions on answers to likely questions, tell staff to say nothing.

The instruction not to speak to anyone about the crisis should certainly be issued to the general staff early on in the crisis, in conjunction with the human resources action team.

Command and control

The crisis management team's role is to direct the media interface but not be directly involved in it. It should seek the advice of the public relations team leader and dictate the line to be taken.

This applies equally to individual enquiries from customers or members of the public.

In most situations, you would expect the crisis management team to accept the public relations team leader's advice – after all, the latter is the expert.

What is important is to make sure that the public relations team are not going to say anything that conflicts with information that the crisis management team may have. The crisis management team leader may also wish to question the public relations team leader on the rationale behind his or her proposals, so that the main team has a full understanding of how the media interface may develop.

Media interface summary

In this chapter, we have covered the following aspects of controlling the media interface during a crisis:

- Media attention.

- Reputational damage.

- Sources of information for the media.

- The front man.

- Media training.

- The media fixer.

- The right messages.

- The official line.

- Command and control.

Things you need to know...

**ORGANISING THE MEDIA INTERFACE
KEY QUESTIONS**

53   What level of media interest will be attracted in the event of a major crisis?

54   What is the risk of reputational damage to the business?

55   How are the above assessments made and are they regularly reviewed?

56   How do we ensure that staff members do not make unauthorised media statements?

57   Is there a nominated media front man? Who?

58   Has the front man received media training?

59   Does our public relations team leader have good relations with the media?

60   Does the public relations team have pre-prepared scripts to cover a range of crisis situations?

61   Are these scripts regularly reviewed to ensure they keep track with business developments?

62   What arrangements exist for getting crisis messages out to all staff members?

63   What is the relationship between the crisis management team and the public relations team in a crisis?

THOROGOOD

PROFESSIONAL

INSIGHTS

Chapter 6

Action teams/plans

Chapter 6
Action teams/plans

Action teams

In previous chapters, we have discussed at some length the role of the crisis management team (CMT) and have referred to 'action teams' from time to time. We have looked at the specific communications requirements of the public relations (PR) and human resources (HR) teams and dealt with the media-handling role of the former in Chapter 5.

As we know, the role of the CMT is one of command and control, so we shall now turn our attention to the people who would be required to 'roll their sleeves up', provide information and carry out instructions, in the event of a crisis.

To this end, every function (other than those deemed to have no emergency role during a crisis) needs to have an established action team.

An action team needs the same things as the CMT:

- A leader.
- A deputy.
- Team members.
- Action plans.
- Somewhere to operate from.
- Access to essentials.

Terms of reference

Action teams are directed by and report to the CMT – their authority stems from it and it is imperative that this fact is acknowledged in each team's terms of reference **and** by line management generally. To recap on the main theme of Chapter 3 on Command and control, the CMT has total control once a crisis has been declared. It would be likely to cause major problems if any other authorities were exercised during such a time.

The hierarchy needs to be as shown in Figure 3, which illustrates a simple crisis management structure. Note that the teams have been divided into three phases. Whilst this reflects the normal invocation sequence of action plans, that is, of course, a matter for the CMT, given the nature and extent of any specific crisis. It should also be borne in mind that, as a major crisis develops, invocation sequences would become blurred, to say the least. This is particularly true of teams that have numerous action plans. For instance, a technology team may have a separate plan for restoring computer facilities to each department: It would not be likely that all would be invoked simultaneously – in fact, it may be impossible due to resource constraints.

It does help, however, to have standardised procedures and approaches, particularly in training sessions and exercises, so that those involved become familiar with what might be termed the 'normal' sequence of events.

It's a bit like driving a manual shift car – whilst you are learning to drive normally, you will move through the gearbox sequentially (1, 2, 3, 4, 5, 4, 3, 2, 1), but as you become more familiar with driving in general, and with the car in particular, you quickly learn that you have to shift gears out of sequence sometimes, to meet prevailing conditions.

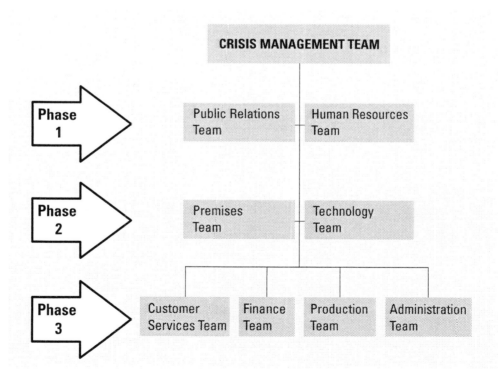

Figure 3: **The Crisis Management Hierarchy**

Action Teams are directed by and report to the Crisis Management Team

Normal action plan invocation sequence

In the early stages of a crisis, the CMT will have two main objectives:

- Ascertain exactly what has happened.

- Prevent unnecessary reputational damage.

Phase 1

In order to achieve these objectives, the CMT will certainly have to activate the Public Relations and Human Resources action teams. Whilst these teams will initially be focused on the prevention of unnecessary reputational damage, it may be that the PR team will be able to use its contacts to get a better insight into the details of the crisis.

The CMT is likely to be totally reliant on the emergency services where the crisis is one involving physical loss or criminal activity, so it will be hard to get independent verification of what has actually happened.

In the case of denial of access to premises, the CMT may decide to send technical team leaders to liase with emergency service representatives on-site, in order to establish the position on the ground and report back. Whilst they are not likely to be allowed to enter restricted areas, they will be more able to assess the damage and its likely effects on the organisation, thus giving the CMT a more informed report. Technical team leaders (in our example, this would refer to Premises and Technology) will be aware that they may be called upon to perform such ad hoc tasks for the CMT **before** their respective action plans are invoked.

Only when the CMT has reliable information, will it be in a position to decide which of the remaining action plans should be invoked and in what order. Until then, it will concentrate on the prevention of unnecessary reputational damage, using the PR and HR teams, as discussed in Chapter 5 on Organising the media interface.

Phase 2

In a physical crisis, once the Phase 1 teams have completed the first phase of their work, the CMT is likely to need to activate the Phase 2 teams (Premises and Technology) to carry out any relocation/remedial works and to put in place an infrastructure to allow the speedy resumption of normal services.

At this stage, the CMT will wish to arrange for all action team leaders not yet involved to be contacted (by and large, this means the Phase 3 team-leaders). They will be given an update on the crisis and how it is being tackled, and will be asked what their problems are likely to be. Effectively, they will be put on standby and it is worth noting that this should mean they would have enough notice to ensure that they have everything they need once their plans are invoked.

This is not a luxury afforded to the CMT or the Phase 1 teams!

Phase 3

Once the CMT has discussed the information obtained from the Phase 3 team-leaders, it will invoke the necessary action plans, giving whatever specific instructions are required, dependent on the nature of the crisis.

Non-essential functions

Every organisation has functions that would be best kept out of the way during the resolution of a crisis. Two that immediately spring to mind are internal audit and compliance, but any function that is purely administrative may well be categorised as non-essential, in crisis terms.

These are functions that are essential to the smooth, efficient running of the business during normal times, but they can add no value to the cut and thrust environment of crisis management.

They are likely to have their own action plans to cover any crisis that directly affects them, but, in isolation, such an event would not be considered a corporate crisis that required invocation of the CMT. If the crisis were part of a wider situation that **did** require such invocation, it is likely that the CMT would leave it to its own devices, requiring only that it did not interfere with essential crisis management efforts.

That is not to say that members of staff employed within these functions have no role to play during a corporate crisis. Internal audit, for instance, is staffed with highly professional people who know something about a great deal of the business. These people represent an ideal resource for bolstering depleted departments or providing additional manpower to clear backlogs or handle crisis bottlenecks in front-line departments.

Where the CMT requires staff resource from non-essential functions, it may expect those functions to postpone implementation of their own crisis action plans for the duration.

Reserve skills register

Many of the more senior people within non-essential functions would have had previous experience in other areas of the business. These people should be included on the reserve skills register held by HR, which would be referred to should the need arise.

In a large organisation, it is imperative that this register is in place and kept up-to-date.

The easiest way to set up the register, in the first instance, is to circularise all managers, asking for details of skill sets previously acquired by them and of any that they are aware of amongst their members of staff. It should be possible to corroborate claims by reference to staff records (application forms, CVs, records of previous positions within the organisation) where this is considered necessary.

Amendment of the register should be an item on HR's appointment and termination checklist.

It's worth stressing, at this point, that the reserve skills register is not likely to contain the names of people who would be the natural first choice to fill a position, should it become vacant. What you need on the register is mature, experienced people who, armed with an up-to-date procedure manual, could perform the essential aspects of the job reasonably well for a limited period of time.

The HR department should consider circularising those on the register (say, annually) to remind them that they are 'earmarked' for certain duties in the event of a corporate crisis.

Where the reserve 'occupation' is critical, it is worth considering short secondments to ensure that the reserve is kept reasonably up-to-date with the function he or she may be asked to assist in.

There exists a well-developed market for interim managers and temporary staff in most business centres, but it is natural to prefer to use your own people, wherever possible, during a corporate crisis.

Action plans

Having discussed the way in which action teams are likely to be activated during a corporate crisis, we now need to look at the way a simple action plan may be structured. Remember that an action team may have a number of action plans, depending on the complexity of the functions it represents.

If you are setting up your crisis management infrastructure for the first time, when looking at action teams and plans, you will need to adopt an approach similar to this:

- Prepare a detailed map of all of your business functions.

- Decide which functions are non-essential (in a crisis) and disregard them for corporate crisis management purposes.

- Allocate the remaining functions to senior managers and contact them to ensure they are the right people and that the functions are correctly drawn.

- Design a pro-forma action plan document, which can be used for every action plan.

- Require the chosen senior managers to submit action plans using the pro-forma document.

- Evaluate the resultant submissions and agree final plans.

- Consolidate the plans into the crisis management manual.

Getting the structure right

Dealing with the first three bullet points in the above list, let's look at the practicalities of getting the functions right and correctly identifying those action plans that need to be set up as **corporate** plans, i.e. those plans that would have a critical significance during a major crisis.

Figure 4 shows the initial results for a simple finance division, with five functions.

It has been decided that the Treasury and Accounts Payable functions are critical and that, accordingly, corporate crisis action plans are required for them. In the first instance, the Chief Financial Officer has been identified as the senior manager responsible for these plans. The remaining functions (Management Accounts, Taxation and Reporting) are not considered critical to the survival of the organisation in the early days of managing a crisis. They will certainly need their own departmental action plans, but these will be considered once the corporate structure is finalised.

Clearly, this organisation regards its credit reputation to be of major significance and recognises that it must service its money market dealings and keep its suppliers happy if it is to get a corporate crisis under control.

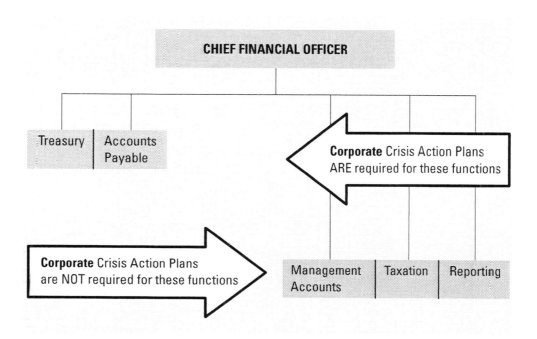

Figure 4: Finance Division's initial action plan structure

It may be that the Chief Financial Officer, on receiving the details allocated to him, will advise that there are, in fact, three functions within Treasury: Front office (dealing), middle office (risk management) and back office (clerical support). He may submit that two action plans are required; one covering the front and back offices, which will be a corporate action plan, and one covering the middle office, which will be a departmental action plan. The Chief Financial Officer may explain that front and back office functions are all that will be required to keep the organisation's day-to-day dealing requirements going and

that middle office staff will thus be free to assist, if required. On the basis that this amendment is approved, the Chief Financial Officer will be instructed to submit an action plan covering the front and back offices only.

Action plan pro-forma

There are two basic reasons why it is essential that a standard pro-forma be used for documenting crisis action plans:

- It forces the creator to consider all elements of the plan.

- It makes it easier for a 'stand-in' leader to find his or her way round it.

It is quite common for people to seek to bypass such a perceived constraint on their creative talents by scribbling **'see attached'** on the pro-forma and attaching a plan that they may have produced in the past. This should not be accepted, for the reasons given in the immediately preceding bullet points.

An example of a corporate crisis action plan pro-forma, completed in respect of the treasury dealing function, as discussed in the previous paragraphs, is given in Appendix 3.

Considering draft action plans

It is suggested that the organisation should set up a crisis project team to deal with the critical appraisal of crisis action plan submissions, if they are being considered for the first time. It is obvious, from the example in Appendix 3, that there needs to be significant interaction between teams for any plans to be successful. Phase 3 teams are particularly reliant upon phase 1 and 2 teams.

All references to interplay with other teams should be cross-referenced to the appropriate action plans of those teams to ensure that there is no disagreement about timescales.

I remember carrying out an audit of a service department's action plan some years ago and finding that the whole plan was predicated on the fact that a full replacement computer service would be provided within 4 hours of being ordered. This was extremely impressive, given the complexities of the computer system involved. The only problem was that, when I looked at the computer department's action plan, that system was listed as taking 4 **days** to replicate.

The whole action plan for that service department had to be checked through and reworked.

It is likely that the example Treasury dealing action plan, in Appendix 3, would require some refinement in other areas.

For instance, under 'Dependencies', the Chief Financial Officer has indicated that a specific sized room is required, but has also stated that the Treasurer's home study would be available, as a last resort. This creates an element of uncertainty, which would build delays into the plan's execution. It would also tie the Premises team up unnecessarily at a time when they could be under significant pressure in other areas. The project team may consider this to be unacceptable and may instruct that the plan be re-submitted on the basis that the Treasurer's home study be the first choice.

The project team may also question the need for a full treasury computer system, in the first instance. The view may be that, if the dealing function can operate successfully for (say) 60 hours using hard copy reports, spreadsheets and simple telephony, then that is what the plan should provide for.

Both of the above changes would result in a more positive approach to the problem, enabling the Finance action team to have a dealing function operational in a much shorter timescale than envisaged in the original submission.

The over-riding requirement would be for the project team to remove all unnecessary complications from action plans and to make them as simple and independent of other teams as possible – **Simple plans are the best**.

Retention of action plans

Approved action plans need to be retained in a number of places. Obviously, the team responsible for executing a particular plan needs to have a copy available to it, as does the crisis management team. It is also appropriate for teams that have a particular responsibility to provide assistance to a plan to have a copy of that plan.

It makes sense to have a crisis management manual, which contains every action plan, available to all those involved in the crisis management effort.

Review of action plans

The final box in the example action plan, in Appendix 3, states that it should be reviewed every year. In some areas, this might be considered too long a period between reviews. If the plan is studied closely, it becomes obvious that there are a number of inbuilt dependencies that could affect it dramatically, were they to change:

- Personnel changes.

- The Treasurer moving to a house without a study.

- Changes to computer systems or operating systems.

- Closure or relocation of a branch.

- Change of bankers.

In addition to regular review, it is useful to include reference to crisis management in the deliverables of every major project. Thus, if there were a project to install a totally new Treasury management computer system, one of the deliverables would be to consider the crisis management implications and review the Treasury dealing action plan accordingly.

Summary of action teams/plans

In this chapter, we have covered the following topics:

- Action teams.

- Terms of reference.

- The crisis management hierarchy.

- Normal action plan invocation sequence.

- Non-essential functions.

- Reserve skills register.

- Getting the action plan structure right.

- Action plan pro-forma.

- Considering draft action plans.

- Retention of action plans.

- Review of action plans.

Things you need to know...

ACTION TEAMS/PLANS
KEY QUESTIONS

64   Which functions have established crisis action teams?

65   Are there Terms of Reference for each team?

66   How are teams graded, in terms of importance to the crisis effort?

67   Which functions are considered 'non-essential' during a crisis?

68   Do non-essential functions have crisis plans of any kind?

69   What arrangements exist for identifying and registering staff with useful 'reserve' skills?

70   How are 'stand-in' staff members kept aware of their obligations in a crisis?

71   What arrangements exist for obtaining outside expertise quickly, if required?

72   Is there a standard crisis action plan document that all teams use?

73   What is the process for independently appraising action plans?

74   Have all action plans been cross-referenced to ensure compatibility with each other?

75   Have all action plans been approved? By whom?

76   Where are copies of action plans kept?

THOROGOOD
PROFESSIONAL
INSIGHTS

Chapter 7

Maintaining the crisis management infrastructure

Chapter 7

Maintaining the crisis management infrastructure

Setting up a crisis management infrastructure, along the lines discussed in preceding chapters, requires a significant amount of investment – the majority of which will be wasted if not properly maintained.

But, what do we mean by 'infrastructure'?

In short, it is the framework that has been set up to deal with a corporate crisis:

- The people who have been allocated specific tasks in the event of a crisis.

- The information that will be needed to activate those people and to help them complete their tasks.

- The equipment and accommodation that must be both available and functional to ensure that the people have the appropriate environment to complete their tasks.

The crisis management manual

This framework should be fully documented in a crisis management manual and it is this manual that needs to be kept up-to-date.

Maintenance of the crisis management infrastructure is an ongoing job. In a large organisation it could be a full-time job for one or more people. In some organisations, the role may be delegated to a risk management department, in others it may be seen largely as a compliance issue. For our purposes, we shall refer to the official responsible as the 'crisis administrator'. It will be his or her task to ensure that the crisis management manual is kept current and that all interested parties have access to the latest version.

By its very nature, the crisis management manual will contain a significant amount of personal and confidential information. It is therefore inappropriate that its updates should be distributed to all staff, as is normally the case with operational procedure manual updates. Senior people, in particular, can become extremely agitated if their private addresses, telephone numbers and partners' first names are made available to all and sundry. The crisis administrator needs a crisis management manual distribution list, formulated on a 'need to know' basis.

Extracts from the manual

In earlier chapters, we have referred to the information that the CMT members need to have available at all times as the 'crisis pack'. This, as well as any other crisis information that is made available, will effectively be an extract from the crisis management manual. It is recommended that it be the crisis administrator's responsibility to ensure that such extracts are kept in line with the manual itself, rather than expecting recipients of the manual to update their own extracts – that will not happen.

Before we go any further, it's worth stressing that maintenance requires considerable effort, which is not confined to the crisis administrator – every department must maintain its part of the infrastructure and the necessary controls must be in place. It is therefore certain that crisis management procedures and controls will feature in most procedure manuals throughout the organisation.

Problem areas

Let's look at a few of the things that will go wrong, if they are not constantly checked:

- **Team Leaders, Deputies and Team Members** – May leave the organisation, retire, be absent on extended sick leave, change jobs within the organisation, acquire conflicting responsibilities, be unaware of their crisis management role.

- **Contact Lists, Communications Cascades** – Telephone numbers may change, people may move office or house, or be affected as indicated above.

- **Action Plans** – Systems and procedures may change, equipment may change, locations may change, dependencies may change, contact names/addresses may change.

- **Crisis Centre** – Location may become inappropriate, key holder details may change, inventory items may be lost, accommodation may not be maintained, security may become lax, location map may become out-of-date.

- **Emergency Information** – May become out-of-date, cease to be produced (not required for operational purposes), become unreliable.

- **Emergency Equipment** – May not be properly maintained, may not function, may be stolen, damaged.

- **Information, Training and Testing** – People forget or become unaware of their responsibilities without constant reminding.

In the remainder of this chapter we shall explore the detail behind each of the above bullet points and offer example control mechanisms for each one.

Team leaders, deputies and team members

Keeping abreast of all the personnel changes that take place in a large organisation can be extremely time-consuming and it is important that as much automation as possible be introduced into the task.

If your crisis management manual is a straightforward word-processed document with no linkages to ensure that any amendment is automatically reflected wherever else the item occurs, it is best to keep all of your contact names and details in one place – an appendix, perhaps. If you adopt this approach, it may be that everybody involved in crisis management will be able to work from the same source, obviating the need for customised lists for different people and cutting down the administrative overheads significantly.

Unfortunately, there is only so far that you can go in simplifying matters. You will always need at least two listings: The first being an alphabetical listing of the roles allocated in a crisis and the second being an alphabetical listing of names.

It is essential that people can be located either way as some people may have more than one role in a crisis, which fact will only reveal itself on the alphabetical names list.

An example extract from the type of list, or contact register, suggested above is given in Appendix 4.

Looking at the example, we can see that John Smith, the CMT Leader. has no other crisis roles. This is indicative of the importance of that particular role. If, however, a crisis was called and John Smith was unavailable, Mary Mary would step in as leader, being the first deputy. In all probability, she would want Albert Champion to join the CMT as the Admin member. This would mean that Albert Champion would not be available to lead the Premises Team, which would need to use its deputy leader (not shown in the example).

Let's now look at the procedures that should be used to ensure that the contact register is kept up-to-date:

1   Personnel records should be flagged to indicate if an employee has a crisis management role.

2   Termination or transfer checklists should include reference to crisis management roles, with any crisis equipment (pagers, etc) being collected on the final day and passed to the crisis administrator.

3   The crisis administrator should be included on the circulation list for schedules of leavers, people who have changed jobs/titles in the organisation and people who have moved house. These schedules should contain the crisis management role flag, where appropriate.

4   The crisis administrator should use the above information to amend existing entries on the contact register, remove people and agree replacement names.

5   The crisis administrator should ensure that all new names on the register receive appropriate information regarding the role assigned to them.

6   Periodically, (say every 3 months) the crisis administrator should send every name on the register an extract of his or her entry together with a request that they (a) confirm that the details are correct, or, (b) return the extract duly amended.

In Chapter 4 on Communications, we discussed the call sequences that would need to be used by a call handling company in contacting the CMT Leader. It was concluded that the instructions to the call company would need to be very precise.

It is likely that the call company would need its own form of contact listing, which would mean that the crisis administrator would have an additional task of ensuring that (a) it was up-to-date each month and (b) an amended version was sent to the call company if there had been any changes.

An alternative approach would be to allocate a number to every name, print that number on the contact register and instruct the call company to contact the numbers, details of which they will find on the standard contact register.

In my experience, it is better to retain a separate name schedule for contacting the CMT Leader (as shown in Figure 2 in Chapter 4 on Communications) as this contact is absolutely vital, and no misunderstandings should be tolerated. Once the leader has been contacted, however, the use of a numbered contact register could well be more practical. It is quicker for the leader to say 'Please contact number 11 to prepare the crisis centre immediately; numbers 5,6 and 7 to go to the crisis centre immediately and numbers 15 and 23 to stand by for my call', than to go through all of the names.

The right team members

The procedures referred to above will ensure that we have the right **details** for our team members and other crisis personnel, but how do we know that we have got the **right team members**?

Periodically, it is necessary to consider this point.

The identity of the CMT Leader and the make up of his team, including deputies, is a matter of great importance to an organisation, and its consideration should be reserved to the Board or a relevant Board Committee (Risk Management or Audit and Compliance, perhaps).

> *I would suggest that the Board/Committee should consider these arrangements each year, on receipt of a report from the crisis administrator, which either recommends the continuation of existing arrangements or suggests amendments, where these can be justified.*

Changing the membership of the CMT should not be contemplated lightly – a great deal of preparation and training would have been invested in the team and any diminution in its state of readiness would be a loss to the organisation. Having said that, there are occasions when changes have to be made: Ill health or impending retirement, for example.

Turning now to Action Team membership, the crisis administrator should obtain the views of the CMT on leadership of each team in the first instance. Once this has been resolved, the newly enfranchised team leaders should be required to confirm the membership of their respective teams. Thus, the procedures will be:

- Annually, following the confirmation of CMT membership by the Board/Committee, the crisis administrator should require the CMT to consider the leadership of each of the crisis action teams and confirm existing appointments or appoint replacements.

- Annually, following the appointment of crisis action team leaders, the crisis administrator should require each leader to consider the membership of his or her team and confirm existing appointments or appoint replacements.

Naturally, the crisis administrator should ensure that any new appointments are provided with the necessary crisis information to enable them to perform their allotted tasks. In some cases, this may include specific training.

External contact lists

We have covered all of the internal contacts in the immediately preceding section – all, that is, except the Chairman and Chief Executive Officer, whose numbers will need to be on a CMT contact schedule.

We now need to look at external contact lists, which should be filed with each action plan. These lists would comprise the suppliers, professional contacts, emergency service contacts, etc, that each team has identified as being relevant to its own specific action plans.

> *Periodically (say every 3 months), the crisis administrator should send a copy of each action team's external contact list to the appropriate team leader, together with a request that they (a) confirm that the details are correct, or, (b) return the contact list duly amended.*

Obviously, it makes sense to stagger the timing of these confirmation requests, as far as possible.

Communications cascades

As we discovered in Chapter 4 on Communications, this represents a simple mechanism for getting messages to all staff members during a crisis.

There would normally be no central record of the cascade – the necessary details would simply be held by each member of staff.

There is, clearly, a great propensity for cascade information to become out-of-date. When a member of staff leaves, or moves between departments, keeping the communications cascade current is not likely to be the first thing that the manager thinks about. Certainly, a junior member of staff will not normally think of the need to tell his or her employer when changing their private telephone number – something that is happening more frequently these days as the more-switched-on members of our society give up their landlines in favour of 'sexier', but less permanent, mobile phone packages.

As discussed earlier, it will help in the constant battle against out-of-date cascade information if each manager is required to certify, as part of a regular control certification process, that the details held by him and his staff are correct. This by itself, however, is not enough.

> *Periodically (say every 6 months), the crisis administrator should send a memorandum to every manager, which stresses the importance of an accurate communications cascade and instructs that they circularise their staff with the details currently held by them, requiring positive confirmation or amendment, as necessary. The memorandum should require that managers respond in writing once they can confirm that the review has been completed.*

Action plans

As we have seen, in Chapter 6 on Action teams/plans, a crisis action plan comprises a number of elements:

- Controlling Action Team.
- Objectives.
- Action Plan Personnel.
- Dependencies.
- Plan Base of Operations.
- Crisis Materials (or Information)*.
- Timetable.
- Review Requirements.

*Crisis Information will include, as an appendix, the external contact lists referred to earlier in this chapter.

We have dealt with 'Controlling Action Team' and 'Action Plan Personnel' in earlier paragraphs.

> *The crisis administrator should contact the action team leader, at the frequency required by the review period for each plan, and request that the objectives, dependencies, base, materials and timetable for the plan be critically reviewed. In the event that there are amendments of any significance to these elements, the leader will also be required to review the personnel element.*

It is, of course, possible that the objectives will change because of changes to the business itself, in which case the team leader will be invited to amend the plan, given that there are different objectives.

> It is essential that any changes to a plan's objectives be approved at the highest level.

The crisis centre

On the basis that we have dealt with crisis information and equipment for the action teams in the above paragraph, we can now concentrate on the crisis centre (i.e. the CMT's base) and the information and equipment that the CMT will need.

We have indicated, in earlier chapters, that the role of the CMT is paramount in our considerations, and this means that the crisis centre must be kept ready at all times, so as to be able to accommodate the CMT at very short notice.

It is essential that the crisis administrator should perform a physical inspection of the centre and its equipment and information regularly, say every 6 months. This inspection should cover the following aspects:

- Access arrangements have not changed and key holders are aware of their responsibilities.

- Rooms are furnished and laid out as per specification with no furniture missing or unserviceable.

- All specified equipment (high- and low-tech) is available and functioning as specified. Particular emphasis should be placed on batteries and the presence of clear user instructions for all high-tech equipment.

- All specified information is held securely and is up-to-date. In particular, the arrangements for refreshing such information should be thoroughly reviewed.

- Heating, lighting, catering and toilet facilities should be checked.

- Nominated support staff are aware of their responsibilities in the event of a crisis, including familiarity with the crisis centre.

Information, training and testing

In earlier chapters, we discussed the need to regularly circularise staff concerning their responsibilities in relation to the crisis notification procedures (which, we suggested, should centre around the staff identity card) and maintenance of the communications cascade.

Formal training is something that should be considered for the crisis administrator and also for the CMT leader and his deputies. There are a number of good courses on the subject of crisis management.

Most of the training will, however, stem from the program of testing that should be put in place. This will be discussed at length in Chapter 8.

Summary of maintaining the crisis management infrastructure

In this chapter, we have covered the following aspects of maintenance:

- The crisis management manual.
- Extracts from the manual.
- Problem areas.
- Team leaders, deputies and team members.
- The right team members.
- External contact lists.
- Communications cascades.
- Action plans.
- The crisis centre.
- Information, training and testing.

Things you need to know...

**MAINTAINING THE CRISIS MANAGEMENT INFRASTRUCTURE
KEY QUESTIONS**

77   Is the crisis management infrastructure documented within a crisis
management manual?

78   Who is responsible for maintaining and distributing the crisis
management manual?

79   What arrangements exist for distributing crisis management
manual updates?

80   If there is crisis information maintained outside the manual, how is it kept
in line with the manual?

81   Is there a crisis management contact register?

82   What arrangements exist for ensuring that the crisis contact register is
up-to-date?

83   What crisis information is held on HR's staff records?

84   What arrangements exist for ensuring that crisis action teams have the
right members?

85   Do crisis action teams have their own external contact lists, and if so,
how and how often are they checked to ensure currency?

86   What arrangements exist for ensuring that communications cascades
are properly maintained?

87   How often, and by whom, are crisis action plan objectives reviewed
and approved?

88   What arrangements exist for periodically checking the validity of crisis
action plans?

89   What arrangements exist for ensuring that the crisis centre is fully
equipped and ready for use at all times?

90   How do we check the make-up and state of readiness of the crisis centre
support team?

Chapter 8

Testing the state of readiness

Chapter 8

Testing the state of readiness

We now have a situation where the crisis management infrastructure is in place and we have a crisis administration function charged with maintaining it. The final raft of assurance involves regular testing of the components of the infrastructure.

The benefits of testing

> *Crisis management is exactly the same as learning to drive a car – there is no substitute for actually doing it.*

Every time you carry out a test, you will find something that needs to be improved. It might be to do with the actual mechanics of a plan, the timescales attached to each element of it, or, more importantly, the way the team members interact with each other. It is amazing how some people's personalities change once they come under pressure, particularly if, at the same time, they find themselves with more power than they have hitherto been used to.

The test plan

A test plan should be constructed which spans a sufficiently long period to enable tests to be carried out at an appropriate frequency. Some simple tests will form part of the maintenance effort, referred to in Chapter 7, and will be scheduled on a regular basis: monthly, quarterly or even half-yearly. Other types of test require significant pre-planning and involve cross-departmental co-operation, perhaps in the form of a full-blown project.

Independent review of the plan

The more complex the test, the less likely you are to want to do it too frequently, if only because it puts a strain on day-to-day operations. On the other hand, the most complex tests are generally the most critical and there can be a tendency to 'keep putting them off', simply because they are so involved. This is a dangerous approach, which is best guarded against by ensuring that the test plan itself is reviewed independently, perhaps by internal audit.

The test plan period

I have generally thought that a 3-year planning cycle is the most appropriate for the majority of businesses. That is not to say that I believe that a 3-year gap between tests is ideal for some components of the crisis management infrastructure, but rather that it is unlikely that all components will be tested in a shorter period. It is worth bearing in mind, in this context, that testing requires a great deal of organisation, generally with limited resources.

Types of test

There are four main types of test: Compliance, Desktop, Full and Acid. Compliance is the simplest type and forms a significant part of the maintenance effort, discussed in the previous chapter.

Let's look at each type in more detail.

Compliance testing

As previously mentioned, compliance testing would normally be performed as part of the ongoing maintenance effort, which would be the responsibility of the crisis administrator. Many aspects of the confirmation-testing program were discussed in Chapter 7.

Each test would be included in the overall test plan schedule, which itself would be maintained by the crisis administrator.

Desktop testing

Basically, this type of test involves presenting a group of people with a scenario and talking through what actions they would take, as if it were a real crisis. Normally, this type of test would be used at, say, one or two year intervals, to test crisis action plans, or the way in which action teams respond to a crisis callout (remembering that action teams can have more than one action plan and are likely to be put on notice before it's known which of those plans need to be invoked.

Desktop testing might be used to test the crisis centre support staff team, whose 'action plan' is likely to be fairly routine and mechanistic (if those terms can be used in a crisis situation).

Desktop testing is normally performed in a fairly benign way, with those being tested receiving adequate notice, so that they can make sure that their particular element of the infrastructure is in place before the test. Whilst operational management will tend to consider crisis testing a waste of time (particularly as they are always extremely busy), the fact that the test plan has Board approval will lend it the status it needs to obtain their acquiescence. Giving them adequate notice will help them schedule the 'lost' time and may well help to create the feeling that 'we are all in this together'.

Of course, it is possible to carry out an unannounced desktop test, but I would counsel caution in this regard. I would almost say that descending on an area for a surprise desktop test should be a last resort, to be contemplated only where you were fairly sure that crisis plans were not being taken seriously. You should use it, in effect as a penalty or punishment 'pour encourager les autres'. One thing you must do is to obtain the authority of the executive or director responsible for the area beforehand. If you do not take this precaution, you run the risk that the crisis administrator will be sent away with his or her credibility in tatters.

Organising a desktop test

So, let's look at how we would conduct a desktop test of a specific action plan. For the sake of continuity and simplicity, let's use the Treasury action plan that we set out in Appendix 3:

- About 6 weeks prior to the intended test date write to the Finance Director advising that an announced Treasury desktop test is to be conducted on (date) at (time) at (location) involving (list personnel) and request his support.

- Having obtained the Finance Director's support, and at least one month before the intended test date, write to the Chief Financial Officer, Chief Accountant and Treasurer, (copy to Finance Director) advising that a desktop test of the treasury action plan is to be carried out on (date) at (time) at (location) and, as members of the Finance Action Team, their presence is required. Require confirmation that they will attend and that they will have available to them any crisis materials/information that they may need. Indicate that if any of them are unavailable they must send their respective deputies. It would help to indicate the expected duration of the test.

- Having obtained the team-members' co-operation, invite observers to attend the test. The Finance Director, internal audit, the action team deputies – all of these could benefit from attending the test. Invitations should make it clear that observers should take no part in the proceedings, unless invited to contribute at specific times.

- Prepare a credible scenario that may be expressed in a few paragraphs and that will be handed to the team members, as the test gets under way.

- Prepare a script of questions to be used by the crisis administration team in conducting the test. Questions should be drafted using the latest version of the action plan, as recorded in the crisis management manual.

- On the day of the test, make sure that the test room is ready before the participants arrive. It is most important that there should be no interruptions and that everybody in the room (except perhaps the Finance Director) should consider themselves unavailable for the duration of the test.

- The test itself should be constructed on a 'question and answer' basis. The facilitator would ask a specific, scripted question and, if the answer was not as expected, subsidiary questions would be asked until the answers steered those being tested back onto the correct line, thus

enabling scripted questions to continue. Deviations from the script, or inappropriate responses, may lead to an acknowledgement that changes or improvements need to be made. As such changes are acknowledged, corrective action should be agreed, to be completed by an agreed date, and this should be recorded for presentation in the test report.

- At the end of the test, the facilitator should recapitulate on the agreed action points and ensure that there is no misunderstanding about them. The parties should then discuss and agree the rating that the facilitator believes is appropriate for the test.

It is important that all tests are subject to standard documentation, so as to ensure a uniform approach to different elements of the infrastructure. This covers everything referred to in the above bullet points, from invitations and notices through to issues and action points and, finally, the report itself.

Full testing

A full test involves physically acting out a scenario, rather than discussing it around a table (as in the case of desktop testing).

On its own (i.e. when it is not part of a composite test – see later), full testing is always benign in nature, all parties being given adequate notice to enable them to prepare for the test.

This type of test is particularly appropriate for technical elements of the crisis management infrastructure – elements where the objective is to ensure that 'mechanical' routines, perhaps supported by complex checklists, really will work when put into practice.

An example of a particularly relevant use of full testing might be in a business that is totally reliant on its mainframe computer system. In such a situation, the business must have standby computer facilities, capable of taking over should the main system crash. These standby facilities might take a number of forms, but the most satisfactory would be for the business to have in place its own 'mirror-image' system that is kept in a state of readiness at all times. Such a strategy involves significant capital expenditure and the business would need to know for certain that such investment had not been wasted. It is all too easy, in the ever-changing world of high technology, for upgrades to the main computer system **not** to be replicated in the standby system. Sometimes this might be for

reasons of budgetary constraint and sometimes the requirement might simply be overlooked. Regular full testing will reveal any shortcomings in the standby system, particularly if the tests extend to running the business live for a period of time on the standby system. Such tests are likely to be extremely complex, involving continuity of service and the maintenance of secure databases. These considerations may dictate that tests be organised within a formal project frame-work with long lead-in times and an execution date timed to coincide with weekends or statutory holiday periods, thus giving enough time to recover the situation if things do not go as planned.

A successful test of this nature will boost confidence enormously in an organisation, but let's keep things in perspective. It should be borne in mind that, in a crisis situation, the crisis management team will regard technical support as a 'given'. If the mainframe switchover action plan is invoked, the CMT will expect to have full service provision within the pre-determined elapsed timescales. There should be no possibility that the switch might not work – regular full testing is essential.

One of the problems with **technical** elements of the crisis management infra-structure is that you are totally reliant on **technical** people – nobody else in the organisation is likely to be knowledgeable enough to give adequate independent assurance. Unless you have been wise enough to employ experienced computer internal auditors, there is a case for instructing external consultants to oversee the first test of this nature and to submit a report on its effectiveness, complete with recommendations for improvements where appropriate.

Having explored the relevance of full testing for technical elements of the infra-structure, we should just look at its relevance for non-technical elements. One of the problems with non-technical full testing is that it may be difficult to achieve the same degree of focus where routines are not fully prescribed.

When testing crisis action teams, for instance, the additional benefits to be derived from a full test may be regarded by some as marginal. It is doubtful that any real advantage would be obtained unless the test involved numerous elements of the infrastructure. If this were not the case, all elements external to the team under test would have to be fabricated, thus detracting from the authenticity of the test and demoting it to the same level as a desktop exercise.

Whatever subject is chosen for a full test, the same rules apply: Full, standard-ised documentation and the presence of a monitor.

Acid testing

An acid test is, in effect, a full test without the advance notice. As such, it is clearly something that should not be entered into lightly – mainly because there is always the risk that it could actually cause a crisis if mismanaged.

So, what would be the objective of carrying out an acid test?

Clearly, it would be to test the mechanisms of the crisis management infrastructure and the people involved in crisis management under duress.

As a result, there is no point in carrying out an acid test until you are sure that the various components of your infrastructure are in place and properly maintained. In other words, the compliance-testing regime should indicate that there are no maintenance problems and the elements that you intend to acid test should have recently undergone successful desktop or full testing, as appropriate.

Why do I make these conditions? It's common sense really.

An acid test will require a substantial amount of organisation involving the synchronisation of several elements of the infrastructure, under conditions of some confidentiality. The last thing you would want would be for the test to fall over, particularly in the early stages, simply because one element was not robust enough.

Unless you are the chief executive officer, you cannot even contemplate an acid test without obtaining authority at the highest level. Such a test is likely to seriously inconvenience senior people and could even affect customer service standards. You will need the full support of your organisation's 'big-hitters' if you are to overcome the indignant protests of senior people who have been 'dragged' from their jobs without any notice.

Having secured that support, the last thing that you would want would be to report that the test did not reach its planned conclusion.

Organising an acid test

We shall now look at the stages involved in organising an acid test, bearing in mind that the initial planning stages will have to be managed confidentially within the crisis administration office. If the crisis administrator does not have adequate resources he may have to seek permission to set up a project team.

The need for an acid test will be determined by reference to the approved test plan document. The plan is likely to be non-specific in terms of set dates for acid tests, purely because the publication of such a date would render the test ineffective. The entry is likely to leave the date to the administrator's discretion, within certain parameters, subject only to it not being scheduled until lower level tests have been conducted.

The following procedure should be followed:

1   Decide upon the elements to be acid tested.

2   Obtain in-principle permission for the test from the appropriate senior officer (likely to be the chief executive officer, who will need to be satisfied of the requirement for, and appropriateness of, the proposed test).

3   If necessary, seek permission for a project team to be set up to administer the test – always take into account the need for confidentiality.

4   Devise and document an appropriate scenario, specifying dates, times and information sources.

5   Specify the boundaries of the test and identify the appropriate linkages to other elements of the crisis management infrastructure.

6   Produce scripts for those linked elements that are not part of the acid test and establish a procedure for making those scripts available.

7   Prepare a schedule of all personnel that will be involved in the test and assess the effect on operations/customer service, bearing in mind the timings of each involvement.

8   Prepare a summarised proposal for the test, reciting the following:

    •   Objective.

    •   Test plan rationale.

    •   Location, timing and duration.

    •   Personnel involved.

    •   Operational/Customer service effects.

9   Submit the proposal to the authorising officer, obtaining a signature, if approval is given.

10   Take whatever steps are possible to guarantee the availability of personnel. This is particularly important where directors or executives are involved, as they are likely to have appointments with external contacts at any time. In fact, judicious enquiry before detailed planning commences may save you both time and face later on. (In the past I have used the ruse of asking the chief executive to require the senior people needed for the test to attend a meeting with him on the proposed test date – a meeting which is cancelled at the last minute, thus ensuring availability.)

The above procedure, adjusted to remove the need for confidentiality, may be used equally well to organise a full test.

Acid testing the crisis management team

Although I have argued that acid testing is not particularly effective for non-technical elements of the infrastructure, the CMT may be regarded as an exception to this.

The CMT lends itself to acid testing because of its high level nature and the fact that it can be self-contained within the crisis centre, although, in all fairness, the only part of such a test that can be truly regarded as an acid test is the activation procedure. Once the team is together at the crisis centre, the presence of facilitators and monitors makes it obvious that a test is being conducted, as opposed to an authentic crisis being under way. So, you would be forgiven for concluding that such a test should be classified as an unannounced full test rather than an acid test – even though the definition of a full test is that it is always 'announced'. This does not invalidate the conduct of the test, because it is absolutely imperative that the CMT activation procedure should be tested under duress. Following the activation with a different type of test is a perfectly acceptable proposal, which ensures that full value is obtained from the testing process. This may be referred to as composite testing.

Composite testing

This normally involves mixing full tests and acid tests in such a way as to obtain maximum benefit with minimum disruption risk.

As adumbrated earlier, a true acid test could have disastrous consequences if mishandled.

> *I have heard a director tell a story of the morning he arrived at his organisation's computer centre and literally 'pulled the plug', saying 'you no longer have a mainframe computer – get round it!' A true acid test and an amusing story – except he never told me how the day developed, so I am unable to tell you whether his actions turned out to be brave or foolhardy.*

The point I am making is that it is hard to believe that many organisations would subject themselves to a true acid test of any major business components.

It is more likely that composite tests will be performed. These are tests in which certain elements may start out as acid tests, but which are supported by other elements that are being tested at a lower level (announced or unannounced full tests). Once a certain point has been reached, all elements revert to full test, as opposed to acid test, status. The message here is that, once you are committed to carrying out a major test, you should 'mix and match' your test types in order to achieve the best possible coverage.

Composite testing of this nature can be extremely complex to organise and will require that those personnel involved in 'announced' elements of the test be brought into the project team early on in the planning process, in order to preserve confidentiality.

Summary of state of readiness

In this chapter we have covered the following aspects of testing the crisis management infrastructure:

- The benefits of testing.
- The test plan.
- Independent review of the test plan.

- The test plan period.

- Compliance testing.

- Desktop testing.

- Organising a desktop test.

- Full testing.

- Acid testing.

- Organising an acid test (or a full test).

- Acid testing the crisis management team.

- Composite testing.

Things you need to know...

**TESTING THE STATE OF READINESS
KEY QUESTIONS**

91   Is there an approved Crisis Management Test Plan?

92   If so, who is responsible for maintaining it?

93   Is the Test Plan subject to independent review?

94   What period of time does the Test Plan cover?

95   Does the Test Plan differentiate between types of test?

96   Is there standard test documentation?

97   What arrangements exist for authorising full or acid tests?

98   Is each test formally reported upon, and, if so, to whom?

99   Is there a formal process for ensuring that test report recommendations are acted upon?

100   What assurance is there that technical tests are properly performed?

THOROGOOD

PROFESSIONAL

INSIGHTS

Appendices

Appendix 1

Crisis management team checklist

1 **Update team members on the nature of the crisis as they arrive at the Crisis Management Centre.**

Give them the information you received from the call company together with timings.

2 **Seek out fuller details.**

Radio, TV, call emergency services – use support staff.

3 **Recap on position as updated and decide whether or not to confirm the crisis.**

Whole team to discuss, particular emphasis on team member(s) most affected.

4 **Contact chief executive officer/chairman and advise of situation. Remind them what their roles are in a crisis.**

They should accept your declaration and give you a free hand. You have access to details of their role.

5 **Agree what further, specific information is required and instruct appropriate action team leaders to investigate and provide concise situation reports.**

Whole team to discuss. You have access to schedules of action teams and their roles. You also have access to their leaders' contact details. Impose time limits for reporting back.

6 **Make initial assessment of likely damage to the business – worst-case scenario. Put appropriate action team leaders on notice.**

Whole team to discuss. Take notice of those members most affected. You have access to contact details.

7 **Activate the public relations team. Advise leader of story so far and ask him to establish what is in public domain. Instruct that a media handling plan be made ready. Request liaison with HR team.**

Be careful! If it isn't public yet you may want it kept confidential as long as possible.

8 **Activate the human resources team. Advise leader of story so far and ask for a report on the likely personnel implications. If there are casualties, obtain, or give, details and liase with PR team leader on corporate line. Report back.**

HR and PR will deal with emotive issues. Your concern is skills availability and notifying staff members so that they know what is expected of them.

9 **Decide whether the crisis management team needs additional resources.**

Be careful! You may inadvertently remove a vital resource from another team.

10 **Liase with emergency service contacts as necessary.**

Establish an early relationship as it may pay dividends later.

11 **Keep updating situation from info coming in.**

Radio, TV, call emergency services – use support staff.

12 **Receive and consider situation reports from action team leaders.**

Whole team to discuss, particular emphasis on team member(s) most affected.

13 **Agree action plans that need invoking and instruct leaders accordingly.**

Whole team to discuss, particular emphasis on team member(s) most affected. You have contact details.

14 **Agree media line with PR team leader and let him go ahead. Impose report-back rules.**

You have access to pre-prepared crisis scripts – use these as a basis for discussion. Whole team to discuss, particular emphasis on team member(s) most affected.

15 **Agree Personnel line with HR team leader and let him go ahead. Impose report-back rules.**

Balance need to know against safety and morale. Whole team to discuss, particular emphasis on team member(s) most affected.

16 **Monitor events and react as necessary. Agree and keep revising milestones to successful completion. Agree the point at which the crisis can be deemed over.**

Start to put a timetable together and monitor progress against it (use support staff).

17 Receive action team reports and re-direct efforts as necessary.

Whole team to discuss, particular emphasis on team member(s) most affected.

18 Keep chief executive officer/chairman informed on progress.

You have full executive authority but if you need to commit 'big bucks' run it by them. (It's useful to have unanimous support from team members in such a case).

19 Consider need to activate crisis management 'B' team and place members on notice.

By now you should know if the crisis will be prolonged and what skills would be most beneficial to the 'B' team.

20 As the crisis develops its nature may change. Keep reviewing your plans and milestones.

Whole team to discuss, particular emphasis on team member(s) most affected.

21 Keep reviewing this checklist to ensure that nothing is missed.

Whole team to discuss, particular emphasis on team member(s) most affected.

22 Agree when crisis is over and return control to line management.

Whole team to discuss, particular emphasis on team member(s) most affected.

Obviously, the extent to which the above checklist can be used will depend upon the type of crisis and when it occurs. Suffice to say that the imposition of a checklist approach to crisis management should focus the minds of team members and keep them on track at a time when they will be under extreme pressure.

Appendix 2

The crisis log

Date_____

CRISIS LOG SHEET No: 00001

Time	I.D.E.A.	Initials
07:30	Full Team convenes (initials of those present)	
07:32	Crisis declaration confirmed	
07:35	Call from police control advising extent of crisis	
07:38	IT, PR, HR Team Leaders contacted to stand-by	
07:40	Chief Exec notified of current position	
07:45	Team decides to call for IT situation report	
07:47	IT leader instructed to provide situation report by 08:15	

Appendix 3
Departmental action plan

Corporate Crisis Action Plan

TEAM

Finance.

PLAN

Treasury Dealing (Front and Back Offices).

OBJECTIVE

To establish a fully operational Treasury dealing function in alternative premises, to timescales that will ensure that the organisation's reputation remains intact. In particular to manage the organisation's liquidity and ensure the timely discharge of commitments.

TEAMLEADER

XXXXXXXX – Chief Financial Officer.

TEAM MEMBERS

YYYYYYYY – Chief Accountant (Deputy Leader). ZZZZZZZZ – Treasurer

DEPENDENCIES

1 **The availability of two experienced dealing staff members, who are familiar with the equipment, and one clerk who is familiar with Treasury work.**

Will contact HR Team to provide reserves if normal staff unavailable.

2 **The availability of suitably furnished accommodation. (Room: 3m x 4m; 3 No desks and chairs; standard stationery supply.**

Will contact Premises Team to establish likelihood of alternative premises being available within timescale.

Last resort: Treasurer's home study (additional furniture requirement: 2 No desks and chairs).

3 **The availability of fully functioning telephony. Hardware and software, to current specifications, is desirable but not essential.**

Will contact Technology Team to provide required telephony (whichever location) and investigate the possibility of full system provision. Minimum requirement: 1 pc set up with Windows 98, spreadsheet and word processing software. Email and Internet also required.

Crisis Action Team Base

Manager's Office, AAAAAAAA branch. Manager is aware of contingency arrangements. Team Leader has contact number for key holder. Each team member has location map and is familiar with routes. Finance Action Team emergency cabinet is in place and maintained.

ACTION PLAN CRISIS MATERIALS

No	Materials	Location
1	Treasury System total daily backup	Will contact Technology Team to make available
2	Treasury Dept's own total backup tapes	In emergency cabinet – refreshed weekly
3	Hard copies of end-of-day positions on liabilities and assets. These show repayment dates and amounts for each deal.	In emergency cabinet – refreshed daily
4	Hard copy authorised counter party schedules. These show dealing limits and contact telephone numbers.	In emergency cabinet – refreshed every three months
5	Full contact details of organisation's bankers and other Treasury suppliers	In emergency cabinet – refreshed every three months
6	Full contact details of CMT and all crisis action teams	In emergency cabinet – refreshed every three months
7	Full contact details of Treasury dealing and clerical staff	Communications cascade held by Treasurer – spare copy in emergency cabinet refreshed every six months

ACTION PLAN TIMETABLE

No	Action	Elapsed time
1	Finance Action Team in position	1 hour from invocation
2	Contact Treasury dealing and clerical staff – instruct to stand by. If necessary contact HR team to find reserves	1 hour 30 minutes from invocation
3	Contact Premises Team and agree base for Treasury dealing	1 hour 30 minutes from invocation
4	Contact Technology Team and ascertain level of support available	1 hour 45 minutes from invocation
5	Treasurer to deliver emergency materials to dealing base and prepare for day's work	1 hour from agreeing location with Premises Team
6	Treasury dealing and clerical staff in place	2 hours from agreeing location with Premises Team. **NB: up to 24 hours if HR cannot find in-house reserves**
7	Computer and telephony installation completed and ready to run	4 hours from agreeing level of support (Timescale imposed by Technology Team)
8	Ascertain current/next day's repayments and check amounts	I hour from Treasurer arriving at base
9	Ascertain organisation's liquidity position for current/next day from bank	I hour from Treasurer arriving at base or at start of business, if later
10	Treasurer to contact PR team to discuss corporate line in discussing crisis with counter parties/bankers.	2 hours from Treasurer arriving at base
11	Treasurer to arrange 24 hour temporary liquidity cover with bankers, if necessary	4 hours from Treasurer arriving at base or at start of business, if later
12	Commence dealing operations – to include rebuttal of rumours concerning ongoing viability of organisation (as agreed with PR team)	1 hour after first dealing staff member arrives at base or at start of business, if later

Plan Submitted by: XXXXXXXX – Chief Financial Officer   Date:_____

Plan Approved by: BBBBBBBB – Finance Director   Date:_____

NB: This Plan must be reviewed within 12 months of the above approval date and at least once a year thereafter.

Appendix 4

The contact register

CRISIS MANAGEMENT CONTACT REGISTER – BY ROLE (ALPHA)

Role	Name	Pager	Telephones	Address	Partner
CMT Deputy Leader (1)	Mary, Mary	789101	H. 324252 O. 627282 M. 930313	7 Acacia Drive Anytown AN1 1AB	Martin
CMT Deputy Leader (2)	Bloggs, Harry	112131	H. 233343 O. 536373 M. 839404	Dunroamin Anytown AN12 2BC	Jennifer
CMT Leader	Smith, John	123456	H. 415161 O. 718192 M. 021222	Sans Souci Anytown AN15 3CD	Janet
CMT Member (Admin)	Mary, Mary	789101	H. 324252 O. 627282 M. 930313	7 Acacia Drive Anytown AN1 1AB	Martin
CMT Member (Admin) Deputy	Champion, Albert	142434	H. 748495 O. 051525 M.354555	1 The Avenue Anytown AN18 4DE	Pamela
CMT Member (Customer Services)	Bloggs, Harry	112131	H. 233343 O. 536373 M. 839404	Dunroamin Anytown AN12 2BC	Jennifer
CMT Member (Customer Svcs) Deputy	Brown, Veronica	445464	H. 657585 O. 96??		

CRISIS MANAGEMENT CONTACT REGISTER – BY NAME

Name	Role	Pager	Telephones	Address	Partner
Bloggs, Harry	CMT Deputy Leader (2) CMT Member (Customer Services)	112131	H. 233343 O. 536373 M. 839404	Dunroamin Anytown AN12 2BC	Jennifer
Brown, Veronica	CMT Member (Customer Svcs) Deputy Customer Services Team Leader	445464	H. 657585 O. 960616 M.263646	2 The Road Anytown AN21 5EF	Richard
Champion, Albert	CMT Member (Admin) Deputy Premises Team Leader	142434	H. 748495 O. 051525 M.354555	1 The Avenue Anytown AN18 4DE	Pamela
Mary, Mary	CMT Deputy Leader (1) CMT Member (Admin)	789101	H. 324252 O. 627282 M. 930313	7 Acacia Drive Anytown AN1 1AB	Martin
Smith, John	CMT Leader	123456	H. 415161 O. 718192	Sans Souci Anytown ᴬᴺ15 3CD	Janet

Appendix 5
Recent corporate crises

US Corporate Scandals – 2001/2002

The world was recently rocked by two headline corporate scandals in the United States – Enron (December 2001) and, even larger, WorldCom (July 2002).

These two scandals had the following things in common:

- Both organisations had significant business viability problems.

- Accounting irregularities concealed the extent of these problems.

- Senior officials in the companies apparently condoned the irregularities.

- External auditors apparently did not act in a timely way to report the irregularities.

The books are still being written on these cases, but the moral seems to be that if you involve yourself in high-risk concealment activities that eventually result in thousands losing their jobs (and millions losing their savings), and then get found out, the best crisis management team in the world will not be able to save the day.

It must have been the worst of all possible coincidences that the external auditor in both cases was Arthur Andersen, then one of the world's 'Big Five' firms of accountants. Immersed in allegations that vital documents had been shredded, the Andersen name became untenable in a profession where reputation is every-thing. At that stage, there really was no way back, but it is reported that Andersen had considered breaking its ties with Enron almost a year before the company filed for bankruptcy. Perhaps a crisis trigger point had been reached (Chapter 2), but for some reason the firm decided to retain its relationship with the company. Had it done otherwise, perhaps the outcome would have been quite different. Had Andersen recognised the Enron crisis early enough, broken its ties with the company and managed it out on the basis of professional integrity above all else, perhaps the firm would have been strong enough to survive the subsequent WorldCom debacle. Unfortunately, we shall never know – the world is now getting used to referring to the 'Big Four' when it speaks of accountancy firms.

The Enron and WorldCom scandals have raised enormous questions regarding the propriety of 'Corporate America' and the reliability of the accountancy profession. Both sectors will have to work very hard to regain the confidence of shareholders and the analysts that advise them.

In closing this example, reference must also be made to the peripheral players involved in these bankruptcies. As this report is being finalised, one British bank, allegedly involved in lending to Enron, is already issuing warnings of its first published loss. How many more will there be? Will they recognise a crisis in the making and act accordingly? We shall see.

Royal & Sun Alliance – 1996

On a fine summer Saturday morning in June 1996, Manchester city centre was devastated by the largest I.R.A. bomb attack on the U.K. mainland. Fortunately there were no fatalities.

Royal Insurance's flagship building, Longridge House, was at the very centre of the explosion and a relatively small number of staff members were working there at the time. Whilst the emergency services had cleared the area of shoppers, they had instructed office workers to stay in the building – 34 Royal staff members were injured in the blast, 2 seriously. Incredibly, the same building had been involved in an earlier bomb attack in 1991, although this had caused little damage. The building, some 80,000 square feet, normally housed 600 members of staff and a number of Royal specialist subsidiaries. There were significant computer facilities at the site.

Royal's business continuity plan was invoked as soon as news of the outrage came through and the crisis management team was convened. The incident became a classic 'denial of access' scenario for the CMT who declared the crisis and handed control over to a 'Control Group', in accordance with the company's plan, to manage recovery.

One of the early problems was to identify those staff members who were in the building at the time – attendance records had been destroyed in the blast. The process of elimination, message gathering and the use of telephone cascade contacts achieved this over a period of time.

During the course of the recovery, the company had to face the following challenges:

- Welfare and counselling facilities for affected members of staff.

- Commissioning pre-arranged back-up computer facilities.

- Immediate alternative telephony and postal delivery arrangements.

- Alternative temporary accommodation.

- Staff transport arrangements to temporary accommodation sites.

- Security of the bomb-site to deter looting.

- Salvage of documentation, equipment and personal effects.

- Maintenance of all records for insurance claim purposes.

The process was not easy and it took a long time, but with a pre-defined contingency plan, good communications and teams that knew their roles and responsibilities, the objective of recovery with the minimum of business disruption was achieved. The various business units moved into more permanent accommodation during the first 2 weeks of August and the Control Group stood down a week later.

Ultimately, Manchester City Council decided that the whole site would be redeveloped as a retail area and Royal and Sun Alliance had to find replacement accommodation. This they did, the new acquisitions being funded from the sale of the Longridge House site and insurance claim proceeds.

Julia Graham, Royal's Risk Manager, who was responsible for co-ordinating the recovery process, knows that the company performed well during the crisis, but she also acknowledges how much more difficult things would have been had the outrage occurred on a normal business day. This crisis was the ultimate acid test of the company's continuity plan and it highlighted the following issues:

- Communicate your Plan, practise it and keep it up-to-date.

- Ensure planning and recovery reflects the company's culture.

- Do not presume too much about staff acquiescence to inconvenience.

- Try to pre-arrange as many services as possible (do not forget loss adjusters).

- Do not try to second-guess the future.

- Ensure roles and responsibilities are known and understood.

- Guard against stress or fatigue going un-noticed.

- Document everything that happens.

- Use specialists and experts wherever possible.

- Be prepared to deal with security breaches.

- Communicate, communicate and communicate – put out clear messages.

Royal and Sun Alliance take business continuity planning very seriously, they have good cause to value it and they know that lightning can strike more than once in the same place. Whilst many elements of their plan are touched upon in this report, the company has made the plan fit the business culture and requirements – essential in any organisation. I particularly like the early renaming of the Crisis Management Team to 'Control Group' – it sends out the message to all involved that the crisis is over and the recovery is under way (and under control).

(The author would like to thank Julia Graham, Risk Manager, Royal and Sun Alliance, for her invaluable help in the preparation of the above example.)

Barings – 1995

This crisis caused the downfall of one of the oldest-established U.K. banks as a direct result of the actions of one employee, Nick Leeson, often described as the 'rogue-trader'.

Leeson had been the bank's 'golden boy' in the Far East. The profitability of his operations helped to secure substantial bonuses at all levels, but this profitability became a mirage as he plunged deeper and deeper into high-risk derivative deals that, eventually, the bank would have no chance of honouring without external support. That support was not forthcoming, and the bank failed – a major scandal for the City of London.

Leeson, like all gamblers, hoped to be able to recover the position, given time.

He was able to perpetrate the fraud that concealed his high-risk deals not only because he was so far away from London, but also because of:

- Ineffective internal controls.

- Lack of internal audit support.

- Lack of management oversight and understanding.

- A general desire to see the results (and attendant bonuses) continue.

In summary, this was a crisis that should have been avoided, as discussed in Chapter 1 on Starting at the beginning – crisis avoidance. It so shocked U.K. financial circles that it changed the direction of future financial services regulation.

Perrier – 1990

Just as people used (and still use) the word 'Hoover' instead of 'vacuum cleaner', 'Perrier' was a popular synonym for 'bottled water' – but no longer.

Perrier's premier position in the bottled water market was founded on consumer acceptance that its product was pure. It follows that any high-level risk assessment carried out by the organisation should have identified that an attack in this area would be so fundamental as to threaten the very survival of the business – a true corporate crisis. requiring swift and decisive action.

In 1990, scientists in the United States alleged that Perrier water contained impurities – not just common or garden impurities, but impurities that could be downright harmful, if taken in sufficient quantity. Perrier's response to this news, which quickly got into the international media, was fragmented and confusing, with a host of differing messages being put out – messages which suggested a number of (sometimes conflicting) reasons for the impurities being found. Public confidence was lost and the brand suffered. Customers in restaurants and bars no longer ask for Perrier, they ask for sparkling water.

It is not easy to judge whether or not the company could have survived this crisis with its market share intact – probably not, as the product was entirely dependent on its purity remaining unquestioned. What we can say, however, is that the adverse effects of the crisis may well have been significantly reduced had such an event been foreseen, planned and tested for:

- Scripts should have been in existence to deal with any rumours of impurity.

- Such rumours should have been pre-defined as 'crisis trigger points'.

- A central, all-powerful crisis management team should have taken charge.

- The 'right message' should have been issued from the centre.

Many of the issues discussed in Chapter 5 on Organising the media interface apply to this example.

THOROGOOD
PROFESSIONAL
INSIGHTS

ISBN 1-854182-08-0

9 781854 182081 >

10-12 Rivington Street London EC2A 3DU

t: 020 7749 4748   **f**: 020 7729 6110

e: info@thorogood.ws   **w**: www.thorogood.ws